KB133309

빵플릭스 1

시즌 1 Episode 12~24

Let's 일빵빵

자막없이 보는 미드 영어

빵플릭스 **1** 시즌 **1** Episode 12~24

2023년 1월 16일 초판 1쇄 발행

지 은 이 ㅣ 이서영
펴 낸 이 ㅣ 서장혁
기   획 ㅣ 일빵빵어학연구소
디 자 인 ㅣ 이가민
마 케 팅 ㅣ 윤정아 최은성

펴 낸 곳 ㅣ 토마토출판사
주   소 ㅣ 서울시 마포구 양화로161 케이스퀘어 727호
T E L ㅣ 1544-5383
홈페이지 ㅣ www.tomato4u.com
E-mail ㅣ support@tomato4u.com
등   록 ㅣ 2012. 1. 11.
I S B N ㅣ 979-11-92603-07-0(14740)
          979-11-90278-76-8(세트)

빵플릭스 1

시즌 1 Episode 12~24

이서영 지음

토마토
출판사

"렛츠일빵빵이
더욱 강력해졌습니다"

기종에 따라 플레이스토어나 앱스토어에서
'일빵빵' 검색 후 어플 다운로드받으시고
매일 업데이트되는 최고의 강의를 들어보세요.

CONTENTS

빵플릭스 1

시즌 1 Episode 12~24

lose track of time

시간 개념을 잊다

> **Rachel** "Hi! Sorry, sorry, we're late, we, uh, kinda just, y'know, **lost track of** time."
>
> **Rachel** "안녕! 미안, 미안, 늦어서 미안, 시간 가는 줄을 몰랐어."

📝 Note

• **be on track** = 올바르게 가다
off track = 옆으로 새다, 탈선하다
be back on track = 다시 올바른 길로 돌아오다

» track :(추적하여) 확인하다(track my progress - 진도 상황 확인)
» lose track : 확인, 인지하지 않다
» lose track of time : 시간이 어떻게 가는지 인지하지 못하다
» keep track of time : 시간을 인지 / 확인하다

🕐 Practice

1 내가 시간 가는 줄 몰랐어. 아마 늦을 것 같아.

2 파티가 너무 재밌어서 시간 가는 줄 몰랐어.

3 우리 절대 늦으면 안 돼. 시간 잘 확인하고 있지?

4 시간을 잘 확인하셨어야죠.

👥 주요 장면 STUDY

Rachel Sorry, sorry we're late, we, uh, kinda just, y'know, **lost track of time**.

Rachel 미안, 미안, 늦어서 미안, 시간 가는 줄을 몰랐어.

Ross But a man can change.

Ross 하지만, 남자는 쉽게 바뀌지.

• lose track of time : 시간 개념을 잊다

get into a weird area
이상한 방향으로(이야기가) 흘러가다

Joey Hey, I'll have you know that Gloria Tribbiani was a handsome woman <u>in her day</u>, alright? You think it's easy <u>giving birth to</u> seven children?

Joey 야, 우리 Gloria Tribbiani 여사님도 한때는 예뻤었어. 알아? 애 일곱 낳는 게 쉬운 줄 알아?

Ross Okay, I think we'<u>re getting into a weird area</u> here.

Ross 좋아, 근데 우리 이야기가 좀 산으로 가는 것 같아.

Note

- **get into** : ~로 접어들다, 들어가다. ❺ **get into college**

- **weird** : 이상한, 특이한, 기이한, 정상적이지 않은 **strange**

  » get into ~ area : ~한 곳으로 들어가다, 접어들다, 흘러가다(물리적 / 비유적)

  » get into a weird area : 이야기가 가지 말아야 할 이상한 곳으로 흘러갈 때, 산으로 갈 때

Practice

1 너 지금 이야기가 이상한 방향으로 흐르는 것 같아.

2 우리 좀 위험한 곳을 건드리는 것 같아.

3 그 이야기는 하지 말자.

4 그 부분은 언급하지 말라고 했잖아!

주요 장면 STUDY

Ross Okay, I'm <u>scum</u>, I'm scum.

Ross 그래, 내가 쓰레기야, 쓰레기.

Joey Ross, how could you let this happen?

Joey Ross, 어떻게 그럴 수 있어?

Ross I don't know, God, I, well, it's not like she's a <u>regular</u> mom, you know? She's, she's sexy, she's···

Ross 모르지, Chandler 엄마가 보통 엄마들하고는 다르시잖아. 그분은 섹시해.

Joey You don't think my mom's sexy?

Joey 그럼, 우리 엄마는 섹시하지 않다는 말이야?

Ross Well, <u>not in the same way</u>.

Ross 그게, 약간 다른 차원이지.

Joey Hey, I'll have you know that Gloria Tribbiani was a handsome woman <u>in her day</u>, alright? You think it's easy <u>giving birth to</u> seven children?

Joey 야, 우리 Gloria Tribbiani 여사님도 한때는 예뻤었어. 알아? 애 일곱 낳는 게 쉬운 줄 알아?

Ross Okay, I think we'<u>re getting into a weird area</u> here.

Ross 좋아, 근데 우리 이야기가 좀 산으로 가는 것 같아.

- scum : 인간쓰레기, 쓰레기같은 인간
- regular : 일반적인, 보통의
- in the same way : 같은 방식으로
- not in the same way : 방식이 다른
- Gloria Tribbiani : 극 중 Joey의 엄마
- in her day : 전성기 시절에, 한 때
- give birth to ~ : ~를 낳다
- get into a weird area : 이상한 방향으로 이야기가 흘러가다, 이야기가 산으로 가다

15

a knockout

(한 눈에 매혹될 정도로) 매력적인 사람

> **Joey** Now, here's a picture of my mother and father on their wedding day. Now you tell me she's not **a knockout.**
>
> **Joey** 여기 우리 부모님 결혼식 사진인데, 말해봐, 이런데도 우리 엄마 진짜 안 이쁘다고?
>
> **Ross** I cannot believe we're having <u>this conversation</u>.
>
> **Ross** 이런 대화를 하고 있다는 게 안 믿긴다.

📋 Note

- **knock someone out** : ~를 넘어뜨리다. 기절하게 하다,(비격식) 깜짝 놀라게 하다.

- **a knockout** :(비격식, slang)(넘어가게 놀랄 정도로) 굉장히 매력적인 사람

🕐 Practice

1 디카프리오는 젊었을 때 정말 멋졌어.

2 그녀는 고등학교 때 정말 예뻤어.

3 내 화장법은 너를 아주 예뻐 보이게 할 거야.

4 와 이 드레스 너무 예쁘다.

- trick : 속임수, 묘수, 장난
- a trick question : 속임수가 있는 질문
- hot : 뜨거운, 화끈한, 흥분되는
- a knockout : 매력적인 사람, 엄청 멋진 사람,

- this conversation : 이런 대화, 이런 종류의 대화
- just try to ~ : 그냥 ~해봐
- picture :   상상하다, 생각하다, 그려보다
- pregnant : 임신한

주요 장면 STUDY

Phoebe Hey, Rach.

Phoebe 저기, Rachel.

Phoebe Hello.

Phoebe 안녕

Monica Hello.

Monica 안녕.

Phoebe Going to the hospital tonight?

Phoebe 오늘 밤에 병원 가?

Monica No, you?

Monica 아니 넌?

Phoebe No, you?

Phoebe 아니, 넌?

Monica You just asked me.

Monica 방금 물어봤잖아.

Phoebe Okay, maybe it was <u>a trick question</u>. Um, Rachel can we do this now?

Phoebe 그래, 그냥 교묘한 질문이었어. Rachel, 지금 시작할까?

Rachel Okay.

Rachel 좋아.

Rachel I am so <u>hot</u>!

Rachel 나 너무 흥분돼!

Joey Now, here's a picture of my mother and father on their wedding day. Now you tell me she's not <u>**a knockout**</u>.

Joey 여기 우리 부모님 결혼식 사진인데, 말해봐, 이런데도 우리 엄마 진짜 안 이쁘다고?

Ross I cannot believe we're having <u>this conversation</u>.

Ross 이런 대화를 하고 있다는 게 안 믿긴다.

Joey Come on, <u>just try to</u> <u>picture</u> her not <u>pregnant</u>, that's all.

Joey 그냥, 우리 엄마가 임신 중이 아니라고 생각해봐. 그게 다야.

mean something

진심으로 말하다

> Coma Guy Alright, I'll call you.
>
> Coma Guy 좋아요. 전화할게요.
>
> Phoebe I don't think **you mean that**.
>
> Phoebe 그 말 진심 아니잖아요.

Note

- **meaning** : 의미

  ex What's the meaning of this word? : 이 단어 의미가 뭐야?

  » mean : 의미를 가지다(~를 의미하다)

  » mean something : 어떠한 의도를 담아 말하다

  ex I mean it : 나 진심이야("I'm serious" or "I'm telling the truth.")

  » Do you mean it? 너 진심이야?

  » What do you mean? 무슨 의도 / 뜻이야?

Practice

1 내가 너 싫다고 한 거 진심 아니야.

2 아무 때나 전화해도 돼. 진심이야.

3 그가 헤어지자고 했지만 나는 진심이 아닌 걸 알아.

4 제발 진심이 아니라고 말해줘.

주요 장면 STUDY

Coma Guy Well, thanks.

Coma Guy 그렇군요, 고마워요.

Monica Oh, my pleasure.

Monica 고맙긴요.

Phoebe You're welcome.

Phoebe 천만에요.

Coma Guy So, I guess I'll <u>see you around</u>.

Coma Guy 그러면, 뭐 언제 또 봐요.

Phoebe What, that's it?

Phoebe 네? 그게 다예요?

Monica See you around！

Monica 또 봐요?

Coma Guy Well, what do you want me to say?

Coma Guy 그럼 무슨 말을 할까요?

Monica Oh, I don't know. Maybe, um, "That was nice?", "Admit something to me?", "I'll call you?"

Monica 잘 모르겠지만, 뭐, "참 친절하시네요" 라든가, "솔직히 말하시죠" 혹은, "전화할게요" 같은 거요?

Coma Guy Alright, I'll call you.

Coma Guy 좋아요. 전화할게요.

Phoebe I don't think **you mean that**.

Phoebe 그 말 진심 아니잖아요.

Monica This is so <u>typical</u>. You know, we give, and we give, and we give. And then, we just <u>get nothing back</u>!

Monica 전형적인 분이네요. 알아요? 우리는 베풀고, 베풀고, 또 베풀었는데, 우리가 받은 건 하나도 없네요.

- see you around : 잘가요, 또 봐요.(일반적으로 헤어질 때 편하게 하는 인사)
- admit : 인정하다, 시인하다, 자백하다
- admit something : 무언가를 자백하다, 시인하다

- you mean that : 당신은 그거 진심이네요.
- typical : 전형적인, 일반적인
- get nothing back : 아무것도 돌려받지 못하다

19

grow up
철들다

Joey No, no. He said "When are you gonna **grow up** and start being a mom?"

Joey 진짜야, Chandler가 이러더라고. "언제 철들어서 엄마다운 엄마가 되실 거예요?"

Ross Wow!

Ross 와우!

 Note

• **grow up**

　❶ (신체적으로) 자라다, 성장하다
　❷ (정신적으로) 성숙해지다, 철들다

⏱ **Practice**

❶ 이제 너도 철들 때가 됐어.

❷ 제발 철 좀 들래.

❸ 언제 철들어서 어른이 될래?

❹ 그는 너무 빨리 철들어버렸어.

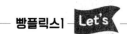
👥 주요 장면 STUDY

Ross Ah, the <u>forbidden</u> love of a man and his door.

Ross 아, 한 남자와 문짝의 금지된 사랑인가.

Joey Shh. He did it. He <u>told her off</u>, and not just about the kiss, about everything.

Joey 쉿, Chandler가 다 말했어. 호통도 치고. 키스 얘기뿐만 아니라 전부다.

Ross You're kidding.

Ross 설마.

Joey No, no. He said "When are you gonna **grow up** and start being a mom?"

Joey 진짜야, Chandler가 이러더라고. "언제 철들어서 엄마다운 엄마가 되실 거에요?"

Ross Wow!

Ross 와우!

Joey Wait, wait, then she came back with the question is, "When are you gonna grow up and <u>realize</u> I <u>have a bomb</u>?"

Joey 그랬더니, Chadler 엄마가 받아치시길 "넌 언제 철들어서 내가 폭탄을 갖고 있다는 걸 깨달을래?"라고 하셨어.

Ross Okay, wait a minute, are you sure she didn't say "When are you gonna grow up and realize I am your mom?"

Ross 그래, 근데, "넌 언제 철들어서 내가 네 엄마라는거 깨달을래?" 아니었을까?

Joey That <u>makes more sense</u>.

Joey 아, 그게 더 말이 된다.

- forbid : 금지하다, 어렵게 하다
- forbidden : 금지된
- tell someone off : ~를 핀잔주다, 호통치다

- grow up : 철들다
- realize : 깨닫다
- make sense : 의미가 통하다, 말이 되다

21

spell something out for someone

일일이 설명해주다

> **Ross** So, what's going on now?
>
> **Ross** 그래서, 지금 상황은 어때?
>
> **Joey** I don't know, I've been standing here **spelling it out for you**! I don't hear anything.
>
> Oh, wait, wait, wait.
>
> **Joey** 나야 모르지, 여기서 계속 너한테 일일이 설명해주고 있었잖아. 아무것도 안 들려. 잠깐, 잠깐.

📋 Note

- **spelling** = 철자, **spell** = 철자를 말하다, 쓰다.

- **spell something out**

  ❶ spell something <u>out</u> : 철자를 알려주다

  i.e Can you spell out 'happy'?

  ❷ spell something <u>out</u> : 상세하게 풀어서 설명해주다.

⏱ Practice

❶ 이 문제에 대해 상세히 설명해주시겠어요?

❷ 처음에는 과정을 상세히 설명해야 해.

❸ 내 기대치를 너에게 일일이 설명해야 하니?

❹ 상황 이해했어. 나한테 설명하지 않아도 돼.

주요 장면 STUDY

Ross So, what's going on now?

Ross 그래서, 지금 상황은 어때?

Joey I don't know, I've been standing here **spelling it out for you**!
I don't hear anything.
Oh, wait, wait, wait.

Joey 나야 모르지, 여기서 계속 너한테 일일이 설명해주고 있었잖아. 아무것도 안 들려.
잠깐, 잠깐.

Ross What did you see?

Ross 뭐 가 보이는데?

Joey <u>Hard to tell</u>, they're so <u>tiny</u> and <u>upside-down</u>. Wait, wait. They're
walking away. they're walking away. No, no they're not, they're
coming right at us! Run! Run!

Joey 잘 모르겠어, 둘 다 작고, 거꾸로 보여. 잠깐만, 잠깐만. 저쪽으로 가고 있는데. 저쪽
으로 가고 있어. 아니다. 우리 쪽이야. 야, 도망쳐!

- spell it out for someone : ~에게 일일이 설명하다
- tell : 구별하다, 식별하다
- hard to tell =It's hard to tell
- tiny : 조그마한, 작은
- upside-down : 거꾸로, 위 아래가 뒤바뀐

go down that road

어떠한 길을 가다

Chandler Pretty good! I told her.

Chandler 제법 괜찮아! 이야기했으니까.

Ross Well, see? So, maybe it wasn't such a bad idea, you know, me kissing your mom, uh? Huh? But, we don't have to **go down that road**.

Ross 그래? 결국 그렇게 나쁜 건 아니었지? 너희 엄마랑 키스한 거 말이야. 응? 응? 하지만, 굳이 꼭 그 길을 갈 필요는 없지.

Note

- **go down** = ~의 방향으로 가다
- **that road** = 특정한 길
  » 특정한 방식대로 일을 처리하다, 어떠한 방향으로 나아가다(*보통은 알면서, 결과 예상해도)
- **go down that road** = 어떤 특정한 길로(방향으로) 가다.

Practice

1 나 그 일을 다시는 겪고 싶지 않아.

2 너는 알면서 또 그 길을 가려고 하고 있어!

3 그 길은 가지 않는 게 좋을 것 같아.

4 그 길을 가기 전에 다른 선택지도 생각해보자.

주요 장면 STUDY

Chandler Hey.

Chandler 야.

Ross You mean that?

Ross 나 말하는 거지?

Chandler Yeah, why not. So I told her.

Chandler 그럼, 당연하지. 다 말씀드렸어.

Ross Yeah? <u>How did it go?</u>

Ross 아, 이땠어?

Chandler <u>Awful. Awful. Couldn't have gone worse.</u>

Chandler 끔찍했지. 끔찍했어. 최악이었어.

Ross Well, how do you feel?

Ross 그래, 넌 기분 어떤데?

Chandler Pretty good! I told her.

Chandler 제법 괜찮아! 이야기했으니까.

Ross Well, see? So, maybe it wasn't such a bad idea, you know, me kissing your mom, uh? Huh? But, we don't have to **go down that road**.

Ross 그래? 결국 그렇게 나쁜 건 아니었지? 너희 엄마랑 키스한 거 말이야. 응? 응? 하지만, 굳이 꼭 그 길을 갈 필요는 없지.

- How did it go? : 어땠어?
- awful : 끔찍한, 지독한
- couldn't have gone worse : 더 나쁠 수는 없다, 최악이다
- go down that road : 특정한 길을 가다, 특정한 결론으로 나아가다

25

a big step

큰 발전, 도약

> **Phoebe** Woo-hoo, first weekend <u>away</u> together!
>
> **Phoebe** 우후, 첫 주말 동반 여행이네.
>
> **Monica** Yeah, **that's a big step**.
>
> **Monica** 와, 정말 큰 발전이네.

 Note

- **a step** = 한 발짝, 발걸음
- **a big step** = 큰 도전 / 도약 / 발전 / 발걸음
- **a big step towards something** = 이루고자 하는 목표를 위한 큰 발전, 모험, 도전

⏱ Practice

1 그건 나한테 큰 도전이었어.

2 네 자신에 대한 이야기를 하는 것이 큰 발전이야.

3 오늘은 우리의 목표를 이루기 위한 큰 도약을 하는 날이야.

4 대학교를 졸업하는 건 어른이 되기 위한 큰 도약이야.

주요 장면 STUDY

Rachel Honey, you can say it, Poconos, Poconos, it's like Poc-O-Nos.

Rachel 자기, 발음할 수 있어. Poconos, Poconos. Poc, O, Nos.라고 해봐,

Paolo Ah, poke a nose, mmm

Paolo 아, Poke A Nose, 음.

Joey, Chandler, and Ross Mma, Mma, Mmaah

Joey, Chandler, and Ross 음, 음, 음

Monica So, did I hear Poconos?

Monica Poconos라고 들은 거 맞지?

Rachel Yes, my sister's giving us <u>her place</u> for the weekend.

Rachel 응, 우리 언니가 주말 동안 자기 집 내어준다고 했어.

Phoebe Woo-hoo, first weekend away together!

Phoebe 우후, 첫 주말 동반 여행이네.

Monica Yeah, **that's a big step**.

Monica 와, 정말 큰 발전이네.

Rachel I know.

Rachel 그러게.

- say : 말하다, 발음하다
- oconos : 펜실베니아에 위치한 캠핑장
- her place : '그녀가 거주하는 곳.' 보통은 '집'을 의미함
- away : 멀리, 떨어진
- a big step : 큰 발전, 큰 도약

27

a fling
썸(진지하지 않은 관계)

Chandler	Ah, it's just a weekend, <u>big deal</u>!
Chandler	아, 그냥 주말이잖아. 별것 아냐.
Ross	<u>Wasn't this supposed to</u> be just **a fling**, huh? Shouldn't it be flung by now?
Ross	그거 그냥 잠깐 썸 아니었어? 지금쯤은 질릴 때여야 하는 거 아닌가?

Note

- **fling**

  1 휘두르다, 내던지다

  2 빠르게 진행되는 행동. 짧은 관계. 가벼운 만남

- **have a fling** : 가벼운 만남을 가지다.

  [한국의 '썸' vs. 미국의 'fling']

  » 썸 : 진지한 관계로 발전하기 전 단계

  » fling : 진지한 관계는 고려하지 않는 단기적인 만남

Practice

1 그들은 그냥 가볍게 만나는 거야.

2 그들은 몇 년 전에 그렇고 그런 사이였어.

3 우리는 사귄 적 없어. 그냥 가벼운 관계였어.

4 나는 한 번도 우리가 가벼운 관계라고 생각한 적 없는데?

주요 장면 STUDY

Chandler Ah, it's just a weekend, <u>big deal</u>!

Chandler 아, 그냥 주말이잖아. 별것 아냐.

Ross <u>Wasn't this supposed to</u> be just a fling, huh? Shouldn't it be flung by now?

Ross 그거 그냥 잠깐 썸 아니었어? 지금쯤은 질릴 때여야 하는 거 아닌가?

Rachel I mean, we are <u>way past</u> the fling thing, I mean, I am feeling things that I've only read about in <u>Danielle Steele</u> books, you know? I mean, when I'm with him, I, just, totally, totally.

Rachel 그러니까, 우리는 썸은 이미 지났고, Danielle Steele 연애 소설에서만 읽었던 그 느낌이 들거든, 그러니까, 그이랑 함께 있으면 난 완전히, 완전히.

Ross <u>Nauseous</u>, I'm <u>physically</u> nauseous. What am I supposed to do, huh? Call <u>immigration</u>? I could call immigration!

Ross 역겨워. 온몸으로 역겨워. 나보고 어쩌라는 거야? 이민국에 전화라도 할까? 그것도 괜찮네.

- big deal : 큰일, no big deal을 줄여서 한 말. 별거 아니야. 대수롭지 않아. = It's no big deal.
- be supposed to ~ : ~하기로 되어 있다
- a fling : 썸, 실컷 즐기기
- fling : 내던지다, 내팽개치다
- be flung : 내팽개쳐지다 내버려지다
- by now : 지금쯤은, 이미
- way past ~ : 훨씬 지난
- Danielle Steele: 미국 유명 소설가
- nauseous : 역겨운, 메스꺼운
- physically : 육체적으로, 물리적으로
- immigration : 이민국

move out
이사하다(현재 집에서 나가다)

> **Chandler** Well, it's a pretty big <u>commitment</u>, I mean, <u>what if</u> one of us wants to **move out**?

> **Chandler** 글쎄, 그건 좀 큰일이라. 무슨 말인가 하면, 만약 우리 중 누구 하나라도 이사 나가게 되면?

> **Joey** Why, are you moving out?

> **Joey** 왜, 이사 가게?

Note

- **move out** : 이사 나가다.
- **move in** : 이사 들어오다.
- **move out day** : 이사 나가는 날
- **move in day** : 이사 들어오는 날

Practice

1 너 이사할 계획이야?

2 집주인이 이번 달까지 방 빼래.

3 한국 사람들은 이사하는 날 짜장면을 먹어.

4 나 얼른 이사하고 싶어.

주요 장면 STUDY

Joey Ok, ok. How about if we <u>split</u> it?

Joey 좋아, 좋아, 우리가 나눠서 내면 어때?

Chandler What do you mean, like, buy it together?

Chandler 무슨 뜻이야? 공동구매 하자는 말이야?

Joey Yeah.

Joey 응.

Chandler You think we're ready for <u>something like that</u>?

Chandler 우리가 그런 걸 할 수 있을까?

Joey Why not?

Joey 그럼.

Chandler Well, it's a pretty big <u>commitment</u>, I mean, <u>what if</u> one of us wants to **move out**?

Chandler 글쎄, 그건 좀 큰일이라. 무슨 말인가 하면, 만약 우리 중 누구 하나라도 이사 나가게 되면?

Joey Why, are you moving out?

Joey 왜, 이사 가게?

Chandler I'm not moving out.

Chandler 이사 안 가.

- split : 나누다
- something like that : 그런 것, 일
- commitment : 약속, 책무가 따르는 일
- what if : 만약 ~하면
- move out : 이사 나가다

out of sorts
몸 또는 기분이 안 좋은

> Monica Phoebe, what's the matter?
>
> Monica Phoebe, 무슨 일이야?
>
> Phoebe Nothing, I'm sorry, I'm just, **I'm out of sorts**.
>
> Phoebe 아무것도 아니야. 미안. 그냥 기분이 좀 안 좋아서 그래.

📖 Note

• **be / feel out of sorts** = 당사자가 몸 또는 기분이 안 좋다.

• **put / make someone out of sorts** = 누군가를 몸 / 기분이 안 좋게 하다.

🕐 Practice

1 나 요즘 기분 / 컨디션이 좀 안 좋아.

2 너 왜 그래? 좀 안 좋아 보여.

3 그 소식이 나를 기분 나쁘게 만들었어.

4 나 요즘 잠을 못 자서 컨디션이 좀 안 좋아.

🎭주요 장면 STUDY

| Rachel | Pheebs! |

| Rachel | Phoebe! |

| Phoebe | Fine! |

| Phoebe | 알겠어! |

| Monica | Phoebe, what's the matter? |

| Monica | Phoebe, 무슨 일이야? |

| Phoebe | Nothing, I'm sorry, I'm just, **I'm out of sorts.** |

| Phoebe | 아무것도 아니야. 미안. 그냥 기분이 좀 안 좋아서 그래. |

| Chandler | Ah, you can use my <u>sorts</u>, I <u>rarely</u> use them. |

| Chandler | 아, 그럼 내 기분 좀 가져가. 나 잘 안 쓰거든. |

| Customer | Hey, can we get some cappuccino over here? |

| Customer | 저기요, 우리 카푸치노는 언제 줘요? |

| Rachel | Oh, right, that's me! |

| Rachel | 아 맞다, 나지! |

- out of sorts : 몸이나 기분이 안 좋은
- sorts : 기분, 정신
- rarely : 좀처럼 ~하지 않는

make a move
행동을 하다(작업을 걸다, 진도를 빼다 등)

> Ross I'm familiar with his work, yes.
>
> Ross 그 녀석 하고 다니는 짓 잘 알지. 응.
>
> Phoebe Well, he **made a move** on me.
>
> Phoebe 그가 나한테 작업을 걸었어.

📋 Note

- **make a move** : 행동을 취하다, 움직임을 취하다.

  ❶일을 진행시켰다. ❷조치를 취했다. ❸작업을 걸다. ❹(사이에서) 신노를 나가다.

🕐 Practice

1️⃣ 이건 옳지 않아. 우리 행동을 취해야 돼.

2️⃣ 우리 너무 늦기 전에 행동을 취해야 돼. .

3️⃣ 그가 진도를 나갔어?

4️⃣ 제가 행동할 때까지 기다리시는 건가요?

주요 장면 STUDY

Joey Hey, Chandler, that table place closes at 7, come on.

Joey Chandler, 가구점이 7시에 닫는대. 가자.

Chandler Fine.

Chandler 그래.

Monica Phoebe, what is it?

Monica Phoebe, 뭔데 그래?

Phoebe All right, you know Paolo?

Phoebe 좋아, Paolo 알지?

Ross I'm familiar with his work, yes.

Ross 그 녀석 하고 다니는 짓 잘 알지. 응.

Phoebe Well, he **made a move** on me.

Phoebe 그가 나한테 작업을 걸었어.

Joey Whoa, store will be open tomorrow!

Joey 아, 가게 내일 열거래.

Chandler More coffee over here, please!

Chandler 커피 더 줄래?

• be familiar with : 잘 알다, 익숙하다
• his work : 그의 일
• make a move : 작업을 걸다, 추근대다
• store : 가게

35

make a pass at someone
수작을 걸다

Rachel	I guess you don't.
Rachel	진짜 그래.
Phoebe	Paolo **made a pass at me**.
Phoebe	Paolo가 나한테 수작 걸었어.

Note

["make a move" vs. "make a pass at"]

》 make a move : 포괄적인 개념으로 남녀 간의 작업 혹은 어떤 일을 진행시키다.

》 make a pass at ~ : 이성적으로 육체적이거나 성적인 관계를 목적으로 수작을 걸다.

Practice

1 아무도 나한테 작업을 건 적은 없어.

2 그가 나한테 작업을 걸다니 믿을 수가 없어.

3 그녀한테 작업을 걸어볼까?

4 그녀가 내 친구에게 작업을 걸었어.

주요 장면 STUDY

Phoebe Um, we haven't known each other for that long a time, and, um, there are three things that you should know about me. One, my friends are the most important thing in my life, two, I never lie, and three, I make the best <u>oatmeal</u> <u>raisin</u> cookies in the world.

Phoebe 음, 우리가 안 지는 얼마 안 됐지만, 네가 나에 대해 알아야 할 게 3가지가 있거든. 하나는, 친구가 내 인생의 전부라는 거. 두 번째, 난 결코 거짓말을 안 한다는 거. 그리고 세 번째는, 나는 세상에서 제일 맛있는 오트밀 건포도 쿠키를 굽는다는 거.

Rachel Ok, thanks Pheebs. Oh my God, why have I never tasted these before?

Rachel 그래, 고마워 Phoebe. 세상에, 내가 왜 진작에 맛보지 않았을까?

Phoebe Oh, I don't make them a lot because I don't think it's <u>fair</u> to the other cookies.

Phoebe 아, 내가 많이는 만들지 않아. 왜냐하면 다른 쿠키들에게 공평하지 않으니까.

Rachel All right, well, you're right, these are the best oatmeal cookies I've ever had.

Rachel 맞네, 네 말이 맞아. 내가 먹어본 쿠키 중에 최고야.

Phoebe Which <u>proves</u> that I never lie.

Phoebe 내가 거짓말 안 한다는 거 알겠지?

Rachel I guess you don't.

Rachel 진짜 그래.

Phoebe Paolo **made a pass at me**.

Phoebe Paolo가 나한테 수작 걸었어.

- oatmeal : 오트밀
- raisin : 건포도
- fair : 공평한, 타당한

- prove : 증명하다
- make a pass at someone : 누군가에게 수작을 걸다

hit on someone

수작 / 작업을 걸다

Rachel No. oh, I feel so stupid! Oh, I think about <u>the other day</u> with you guys and I was all "Oh, Paolo, he's so great, he makes me feel so." Oh, God, I'm so <u>embarrassed</u>!

Rachel 아니! 아 정말 바보가 된 기분이야! 며칠 전에 친구들 앞에서 '오, Paolo, 정말 멋지지 않니?' 그랬잖아. 아 너무 창피하다.

Phoebe I'm so embarrassed, I'm the one **he hit on**!

Phoebe 내가 더 창피하지. 그가 수작 건 건 난데.

Note

• hit on = 한번 쳐보는 것(꼬시다, 집적거리다, 작업걸다)

[make a move vs. make a pass at vs. hit on]

» make a move : 가장 포괄적. 상황에 맞는 행동을 취하다.
» make a pass at ~ : 어떤 이성적 관계 또는 성관계를 목적으로 작업을 걸다.
» hit on someone = make a pass at someone와 거의 비슷

Practice

1 그가 나한테 작업 걸었어.

2 그가 너한테도 작업을 걸었어?

3 그는 그녀에게 작년부터 집적대고 있어.

4 제발 그만 좀 집적대실래요?

🎧 주요 장면 STUDY

Phoebe Are you okay?

Phoebe 괜찮니?

Rachel I need some milk.

Rachel 우유 좀 마셔야겠어.

Phoebe Ok, I've got milk. Here you go. Oh! Better?

Phoebe 좋아, 우유 있어. 여기. 좀 나아졌어?

Rachel No, oh, I feel so stupid! Oh, I think about the other day with you guys and I was all "Oh, Paolo, he's so great, he makes me feel so." Oh, God, I'm so embarrassed!

Rachel 아니! 아 정말 바보가 된 기분이야! 며칠 전에 친구들 앞에서 '오, Paolo, 정말 멋지지 않니?' 그랬잖아. 아 너무 창피하다.

Phoebe I'm so embarrassed, I'm the one he hit on!

Phoebe 내가 더 창피하지. 그가 수작 건 건 난데.

• the other day : 며칠 전에

• embarrassed : 쑥스러운, 어색한, 당황스러운

• hit on someone : 누구에게 수작을 걸다, 작업을 걸다

39

a pig

많이 먹는, 더러운, 무례한, 말 안 듣는, 문란한 사람

Rachel I don't know, right, **he's the pig**!

Rachel 몰라, 맞아, 그 녀석이 나쁜 건데.

Phoebe Such a pig!

Phoebe 정말 나쁜 놈이지.

Note

• pig
 » (한국) 많이 먹는 사람, 뚱뚱한 사람, 지저분한 사람
 » (미국) 무례한 사람, 무식하고 고집이 센 사람, 욕심이 많은 사람, 문란한 남성

Practice

1 미안하지만 네 남자친구는 문란한 사람이야.

2 너 문란하게 사는 거 정말 그만해야 해.

3 너 문란하다고 말한 적 없어.

4 모두가 네가 문란하다고 생각해.

주요 장면 STUDY

Rachel Pheebs, if I had never met him this never would have happened!

Rachel Phoebe, 내가 만약에 그를 만나지 않았다면, 이런 일은 일어나지 않았을 거야.

Rachel and Phoebe I'm so sorry! No I'm sorry! No I'm sorry! No I'm sorry!

Rachel and Phoebe 내가 미안해! 아냐 내가 미안한 거야! 아니야 내가 더 미안해. 미안해!

Phoebe Oh, wait, oh, what are we sorry about?

Phoebe 잠깐, 왜 우리가 사과하는거지?

Rachel I don't know, right, **he's the pig**!

Rachel 몰라, 맞아, 그 녀석이 나쁜 건데.

Phoebe Such a pig!

Phoebe 정말 나쁜 놈이지.

Rachel Oh, God, he's such a pig,

Rachel 아, 정말 문란한 놈이지.

Phoebe Oh he's like a.

Phoebe 아, 그 녀석은.

Rachel He's like a big disgusting.

Rachel 그놈은 아주 역겨운 놈이야.

Phoebe like a.

Phoebe 마치.

Rachel pig, pig man!

Rachel 돼지, 그냥 돼지 같은 놈.

Phoebe Yes, good! Ok.

Phoebe 그래 그거야.

• the pig : 역겨운 인간, 문란한 인간, 나쁜 인간
• such a : 정말, 아주
• disgusting : 역겨운, 구역질 나는

41

be there for someone

곁에 있어주다

Chandler "She's distraught. You**'re there for** her."

"완전 좌절하고 있을 때 네가 곁에 있어주는 거야."

 Note

- **be somewhere** = 어떤 장소에 존재하다
- **be there** = '그곳'에 있다 / 곁에 있어주다.
- **be there for someone** = ~를 위해 곁에 있어주다.

⏱ **Practice**

1 나는 항상 너의 곁에 있을게.

2 네가 친구가 필요할 때 내가 항상 곁에 있어줄게.

3 네가 내 곁에 항상 있어줬었어.

4 내가 힘든 시간을 겪을 때 네가 내 옆에 있어주었어.

주요 장면 STUDY

Chandler She's <u>distraught</u>. **You're there for her**. You <u>pick up the pieces</u>, and then you <u>usher</u> in the age of Ross!

Chandler 완전 좌절하고 있을 때 네가 곁에 있어주는 거야. 마음을 추스르게 하고, 이제 Ross 의 시대로 안내하는 거야!

- distraught : 제정신이 아닌, 완전히 좌절한
- be there for ~ : ~곁에 있어주다
- pick up the pieces : 충격으로 산산이 난 조각들을 줍다, 마음을 추스려 정상을 되찾게 하다
- usher : 안내하다
- in the age of : ~의 시대로

43

deserve something

~를 받을 만하다

> **Ross** Come here. Listen, **you deserve so much better than him**. you know, I mean, you, you, you should be with a guy who knows <u>what he has</u> when he has you.
>
> **Ross** 이리 와. 있지, 그에게는 네가 과분해. 그러니까, 넌, 넌, 네가 얼마나 좋은 여자인 지 알아주는 남자를 만나야 해.
>
> **Rachel** Oh, Ross.
>
> **Rachel** 아, Ross.

Note

- **You deserve it.**
  - **1** 좋은 일에는 '당연히 받을 만해'
  - **2** 나쁜 일에는 '네가 초래한 일이야' / '자업자득이야'

- **You don't deserve this.**
  - **1** 나쁜 일에는 '네가 겪을 일이 아닌데'
  - **2** 좋은 일에는 '이 일은 너한테는 과분해' / '운이 좋네'

Practice

1 당신은 정말 큰 보상을 받아 마땅해요.

2 당신 정말 열심히 일했잖아요. 그거 완전 받아 마땅해요.

3 이런 큰 사랑은 저한테는 과분해요.

4 너는 정말 나한테는 과분한 사람이야.

주요 장면 STUDY

Ross Come here. Listen, **you deserve so much better than him**. you know, I mean, you, you, you should be with a guy who knows <u>what he has</u> when he has you.

Ross 이리 와. 있지, 그에게는 네가 과분해. 그러니까, 넌, 넌, 네가 얼마나 좋은 여자인지 알아주는 남자를 만나야 해.

Rachel Oh, Ross.

Rachel 아, Ross.

Ross What?

Ross 왜?

Rachel I <u>am so sick of</u> guys. I don't wanna look at another guy, I don't wanna think about another guy, I don't even wanna be near another guy.

Rachel 이제 남자 질렸어. 남자는 꼴보기도 싫어. 남자 생각도 하기 싫고 남자 근처에도 가고 싶지 않아.

Ross Huh.

Ross 아.

• deserve : ~를 받을 만하다, ~자격이 있다
• what he has : 그가 가진 것, 그가 가진 소중한 것
• be sick of : 질리다, 싫증나다

45

only child
외동

> **Roger** I mean hey! I just met you, I <u>don't know you from Adam</u>.
>
> **Only child**, right? Parents divorced before you hit puberty.
>
> **Roger** 그러니까요, 제가 방금 만났잖아요. 난 당신을 전혀 몰라요. 외동이죠? 사춘기 전에 부모가 이혼했고요?

 Note

- **only child** : 외동

- **siblings** = 형제자매(**brothers**, **sisters**)

  i.e Do you have any siblings? : 형제 있으세요?

  No, I'm an only child. : 아뇨, 외동이에요.

Practice

1 외동인 건 가끔 좀 외로워요.

2 저는 외동인 게 좋아요.

3 나는 항상 외동이고 싶었어.

4 나는 외동이어서 부모님 관심을 독차지했어.

주요 장면 STUDY

Roger I mean hey! I just met you, I <u>don't know you from Adam</u>.

Only child, right? Parents divorced before you hit puberty.

Roger 그러니까요, 제가 방금 만났잖아요. 난 당신을 전혀 몰라요. 외동이죠? 사춘기 전에 부모가 이혼했고요?

Chandler Uh huh, how did you know that?

Chandler 어떻게 알았어요?

Roger It's <u>textbook</u>.

Roger 티가 나잖아요

- not know ~ from Adam : ~를 전혀 모르다
- only child : 외동
- divorce : 이혼하다
- puberty : 사춘기
- hit puberty : 사춘기가 되다, 사춘기를 겪다
- textbook : 교과서, 교과서적인, 모범 답안인

47

better off

~하는 것이 낫다

> **Monica** Hey, how long are you in the city?

> **Monica** 뉴욕에 얼마나 계실 거예요?

> **Mr. Tribbiani** Just for a couple of days. I got a job midtown. I figure **I'm better off** staying with the kid than <u>hauling</u> my ass <u>back and forth</u> on the ferry. I don't know this one.

> **Mr. Tribbiani** 며칠 동안만. 미드타운에 일자리가 생겼거든. 페리 타고 왔다 갔다 하는 것보다 아들과 있는 게 낫겠다 싶어서. 못 보던 얼굴이 있네.

 Note

• **I figure** : 생각해보니까, 결론짓기로(figure out = 생각을 해내다)

• **better off** = '경제적인 상황이 더 낫다'라는 표현에서 주로 사용한다.

  » I'm better off ~ : ~하는 게 / ~인 상태가 더 낫다.
  » I'm better off now. :(내 경제적인 처지가) 이제는 좀 나아졌다.

Practice

1 나는 작년보다 올해 훨씬 더 나아졌어.

2 나는 그 사람이 없는 게 더 나은 것 같아.

3 너는 혼자 사는 게 더 나을 것 같아.

4 네가 일을 좀 하면 살림살이가 좀 나아질 거 같아.

👥 주요 장면 STUDY

Joey Hey you guys. Hey, you all know my dad, right?

Joey 애들아, 너희 우리 아빠 알지?

All Hey! Hey, Mr. Trib!

All 안녕하세요! Tribbiani 씨.

Monica Hey, how long are you in the city?

Monica 뉴욕에 얼마나 계실 거예요?

Mr. Tribbiani Just for a couple of days. I got a job midtown. I figure **I'm better off** staying with the kid than <u>hauling</u> my ass <u>back and forth</u> on the ferry. I don't know this one.

Mr. Tribbiani 며칠 동안만. 미드타운에 일자리가 생겼거든. 페리 타고 왔다 갔다 하는 것보다 아들과 있는 게 낫겠다 싶어서. 못 보던 얼굴이 있네.

Phoebe Oh, this is my friend Roger.

Phoebe 아, 제 남자친구 Roger예요.

Roger Hi.

Roger 안녕하세요.

Mr. Tribbiani Hey, hey. Good to meet you, Roger.

Mr. Tribbiani 만나서 반갑네. Roger.

Roger You too, sir.

Roger 저도요.

Mr. Tribbiani What happened to the, uh, <u>puppet</u> guy?

Mr. Tribbiani 인형극 한다는 친구는 어쩌고?

- be better off : ~하는 것이 낫다
- be better off A than B : B보다는 A가 낫다
- haul : 무거운 몸을 간신히 움직이다, 끌다
- back and forth : 왔다 갔다
- ferry : 페리, 선박
- puppet : 인형, 꼭두각시

49

big time

엄청나게, 대단히, 완전히

> **Mr.Tribbiani** Joe, your dad's in love **big time**. And the worst part of it is, it's with two different women.
>
> **Mr.Tribbiani** 얘야, 아빠가 완전히 사랑에 빠졌단다. 좀 안 좋은 건, 두 여자하고 라는 거지.
>
> **Joey** Oh man. Please tell me one of them is Ma.
>
> **Joey** 세상에, 그래도 둘 중에 하나는 엄마죠?

 Note

• **big time**

1 유명한, 성공한
>> He is now a big time actor.
>> She is a big time musician.

2 굉장히, 엄청나게, 대단히 : 문장 끝에서 강조
>> Your dad is in love. : 아빠가 사랑에 빠졌어.
>> Your dad is in love big time. : 아빠가 완전히 사랑에 빠졌어.

Practice

1 내가 너한테 너무 큰 빚을 졌어.

2 그들은 그 공연을 완전히 망쳐버렸어.

3 그 팀은 그 경기에서 완전히 패배했어.

4 나는 너랑 완전히 사랑에 빠졌어.

주요 장면 STUDY

Mr. Tribbiani Joe, your dad's in love **big time**. And the worst part of it is, it's with two different women.

Mr. Tribbiani 얘야, 아빠가 완전히 사랑에 빠졌단다. 좀 안 좋은 건, 두 여자하고 라는 거지.

Joey Oh man. Please tell me one of them is Ma.

Joey 세상에, 그래도 둘 중에 하나는 엄마죠?

Mr. Tribbiani Of course, course one of them is Ma. What's the matter with you?

Mr. Tribbiani 물론이지. 그중 하나는 네 엄미지. 지금 제정신이냐?

• big time : 엄청나게, 대단히, 완전히

suck up to someone

아부하다, 비위를 맞추다

> **Monica** Y'know what, I mean, <u>all these years</u>, I thought you were <u>on my side</u>. But maybe what you were doing was **sucking up to** Mom and Dad so they'd <u>keep liking</u> you better!
>
> **Monica** 있지, 이만큼 세월 동안 난 오빠가 내 편인 줄 알았는데, 이제 보니, 부모님이 오빠를 더 좋아하게끔 부모님한테 아부만 한 거였네.

Note

- **suck(something) up** : 빨아들이다.(suck up air, suck up dust)

- **suck It up** :(불평하지 말고) 그냥 받아들여.

- **suck up to someone** : ~에게 아부하다, ~에게 비위를 맞춰서 행동하다.

Practice

1 그는 상사한테 항상 아부를 해.

2 나 당신이 그한테 아부하는 걸 봤어요.

3 저는 다른 사람한테 아부하는 거 안 좋아해요.

4 나는 절대 다른 사람한테 아부하지 않을 거예요.

🗣 주요 장면 STUDY

Ross That, that's <u>ridiculous</u>! I don't feel <u>guilty</u> for her <u>failure</u>!

Ross 그건 말도 안 돼. 동생 실패에 왜 내가 책임을 느껴?

Monica Oh! So you think I'm a failure!

Monica 아! 그럼 내가 실패자라고 생각하는거야?

Phoebe Isn't he good?

Phoebe 멋지지 않니?

Ross Yeah, no, no, no, that, that's not what I was saying.

Ross 그래, 아니, 아니, 아니 내 말은 그게 아니고.

Monica Y'know what, I mean, <u>all these years</u>, I thought you were <u>on my side</u>. But maybe what you were doing was **sucking up to** Mom and Dad so they'd <u>keep liking</u> you better!

Monica 있지, 이만큼 세월 동안 난 오빠가 내 편인 줄 알았는데, 이제 보니, 부모님이 오빠를 더 좋아하게끔 부모님한테 아부만 한 거였네.

Ross Hey, I married a lesbian to make you look good!

Ross 야, 너 잘나 보이게 하려고 내가 레즈비언하고 결혼했다!

- ridiculous : 웃기는, 말도 안 되는
- guilty : 죄책감이 드는, 유죄의
- failure : 실패, 실패자
- all these years : 이만큼의 세월 동안
- on my side : 내 편
- suck up to ~ : ~에게 아부하다 비위를 맞추다
- keep ~ing : 계속 ~하다, 지속해서 ~하다

keep an eye on someone

예의 주시하다, 감시하다

> **Joey** If you go to a hotel, you'll be doing stuff. I want you right here where I can **keep an eye on you**.
>
> **Joey** 호텔 가시면, 그런 거 하실 거잖아요. 제가 잘 감시하게 여기 계세요.
>
> **Mr. Tribbiani** You're gonna keep an eye on us?
>
> **Mr. Tribbiani** 우리를 감시하겠다고?

 Note

• **keep an eye on someone**

 1 신경 쓰고 있다.

 2 관심 갖고 있다.

 3 감시하고 있다.

 i.e **I'm keeping my eye on something.** : 나 ~를 예의 주시하고 있어.

Practice

1 제 가방 좀 봐주실 수 있을까요?

2 저희 아이 좀 잠깐 봐주실 수 있을까요?

3 내가 너를 감시하고 / 예의 주시하고 있어.

4 나는 요즘 기술 시장을 주시하고 있어.

👥 주요 장면 STUDY

Ronni Look, I uh, I shouldn't have come. I, I'd better get going, I don't wanna <u>miss</u> the last train.

Ronni 제가 괜히 왔나봐요. 그만 가볼게요. 마지막 기차 놓치면 안 돼요.

Mr. Tribbiani No, no, I don't want you taking <u>that thing</u>.

Mr. Tribbiani 아니, 아니, 그렇게 하고 싶지 않아.

Ronni Oh, where am I gonna stay, here?

Ronni 아, 그럼 여기 있을까요?

Joey Whoah ho.

Joey 워허!

Mr. Tribbiani We'll go to a hotel.

Mr. Tribbiani 호텔로 갑시다.

Ronni We'll go to a hotel.

Ronni 호텔로 가요.

Joey No you won't.

Joey 안 돼요.

Ronni No we won't.

Ronni 안 된대요.

Joey If you go to a hotel, you'll be doing stuff. I want you right here where I can keep **an eye on you**.

Joey 호텔 가시면, 그런 거 하실 거잖아요. 제가 잘 감시하게 여기 계세요.

Mr. Tribbiani You're gonna keep an eye on us?

Mr. Tribbiani 우리를 감시하겠다고?

Joey That's right, mister, and I don't care how old you are, <u>as long as</u> you're <u>under my roof</u>, you're gonna live <u>by my rules</u>.

Joey 맞아요, 아버지. 나이가 무슨 상관이에요. 제 집에 계시는 한, 제 규칙을 따라주세요.

- miss : 놓치다
- keep an eye on ~ : ~를 감시하다, 예의 주시하다
- as long as : ~하는 한
- under my roof : 내 집에 있는, 거주하는
- * by my rules : 제 규칙대로

come clean with someone
솔직하게 털어놓다

> Mr. Tribbiani I can't do that!
>
> Mr. Tribbiani 그건 안 돼.
>
> Joey **Then you gotta come clean with Ma!** This is not right!
>
> Joey 그러면 엄마한테 솔직하게 털어놓든가요! 이건 옳지 않잖아요.

Note

- **come clean** : 깨끗한,(거짓 없는, 감추는 것이 없는) 상태로 오다

- **come clean with someone** = 상대에게 거짓 없이 진실을 털어놓다.

Practice

1 당신이 한 번도 나한테 솔직하지 않았다고 생각해.

2 나한테 솔직하게 털어놓아 줬으면 좋겠어.

3 나는 당신이 솔직하게 털어놓기를 기다리고 있어.

4 가끔은 가까운 관계일수록 솔직하기가 힘들 수도 있어요.

👥 주요 장면 STUDY

Joey Okay. Now this is just for tonight. Starting tomorrow, you gotta make a change. Six years is long enough.

Joey 좋아요, 오늘뿐이에요. 내일부터는 바꾸셔야 해요. 6년이면 충분했잖아요.

Mr. Tribbiani What kind of change?

Mr. Tribbiani 뭘 바꿔?

Joey Well, <u>either</u> you <u>break it off with</u> Ronni.

Joey Ronni 아줌마랑 헤어지든가.

Mr. Tribbiani I can't do that!

Mr. Tribbiani 그건 안 돼.

Joey **Then you gotta come clean with Ma**! This is not right!

Joey 그러면 엄마한테 솔직하게 털어놓든가요! 이건 옳지 않잖아요.

Mr. Tribbiani Yeah, but this is.

Mr. Tribbiani 그래, 하지만.

Joey I don't wanna hear it! Now go to my room!

Joey 듣고 싶지 않아요. 방으로 들어가세요!

- starting : ~부터 시작해서, ~부터
- make a change : 변경하다, 바꾸다
- either : ~하든가
- break it off with ~ : ~와 헤어지다
- come clean with ~ : ~에게 솔직히 털어놓다

all over someone

~에게 관심을 주다

> Chandler Hey, you're not him. You're you. When they **were all over you** to go into your father's <u>pipe-fitting</u> business, did you <u>cave</u>?
>
> Chandler 야, 넌 아버지가 아니야. 너는 그냥 너야. 사람들이 아버지 배관 사업 물려받으라고 했을 때, 결국 했어?
>
> Joey No.
>
> Joey 아니.

Note

• **be all over someone**

1 누군가에게 과하게 관심을 주다. 부담이나 강요를 주다.
2 이성 간에 관심을 가지고 만지거나 집적대다.

Practice

1 그녀가 문에서 나왔을 때 기자들이 그녀를 다 에워쌌어.

2 그들이 사건의 진상을 알아내기 위해 나를 에워쌌을 때 무서웠어.

3 그녀는 파티에서 그한테 스킨십을 계속했어.

4 나는 네가 그녀한테 스킨십 하는 걸 보고 싶지 않아.

👥 주요 장면 STUDY

Chandler Hey, you're not him. You're you. When they **were all over you** to <u>go into</u> your father's <u>pipe-fitting</u> business, did you <u>cave</u>?

Chandler 야, 넌 아버지가 아니야. 너는 그냥 너야. 사람들이 아버지 배관 사업 물려받으라고 했을 때, 결국 했어?

Joey No.

Joey 아니.

Chandler No. You decided to go into the <u>out-of-work</u> actor business. And that wasn't easy, but you did it!

Chandler 아니지. 넌 백수인 배우 사업을 시작했잖아. 그게 쉽지는 않았겠지만, 넌 했잖아.

- be all over someone : 누구에게 과한 관심을 주다, 부담을 주다, 귀찮게 하다
- go into : ~에 들어가다, ~를 하기 시작하다
- pipe-fitting : 배관 공사
- cave : 😀 동굴 / 😀 반대하던 것을 포기하다, 굴복하다
- out of work : 일이 아닌, 실직한, 백수인

end up

(결국) ~하게 되다

Chandler If I turn into my parents, I'll either be an <u>alcoholic</u> blond <u>chasing after</u> twenty-year-old boys, or I'll **end up** like my mom.

Chandler 내가 만약 우리 부모처럼 된다면, 스무 살 소년을 따라다니는 술주정뱅이 금발이거나, 아니면 결국 우리 엄마처럼 되겠지.

📝 Note

• **end up** : 내 의지와는 상관없이 결국 ~하게 되었다.

• **end up doing something** : 결국 ~ 행동을 하게 되다.

• **end up like someone** : 결국 ~와 비슷하게 되다.

• **end up with someone** : 결국 ~와 함께하게 되다.(사람)

• **end up at a place** : 결국 ~장소에 가게 되다.(장소)

⏱ Practice

① 우리는 결국 시골로 이사 가게 됐어.

② 나는 너처럼 되고 싶지 않아.

③ 나는 너희가 결국 함께하게 될 줄 알았어.

④ 그의 음식은 결국 쓰레기통에 버려졌어.

주요 장면 STUDY

Ross So Joey, you okay?

Ross 그래서 Joey, 괜찮아?

Joey Yeah, I guess. It's just, you know, they're parents, after <u>a certain point</u>, you gotta <u>let go</u>. <u>Even if</u> you know better, you've gotta let them make their own mistakes.

Joey 응, 그런 거 같아. 그냥, 부모님이잖아. 어떤 시점이 되면, 놔드려야 하는 거야. 너희들이 더 잘 알고 있더라도 그냥 실수하게 놔두는 거라고.

Rachel Just think, in a couple of years we get to turn into them.

Rachel 생각해봐, 몇 년 후에는 우리도 부모님들처럼 될 거야.

Chandler If I turn into my parents, I'll either be an <u>alcoholic</u> blond <u>chasing after</u> twenty-year-old boys, or I'll **end up** like my mom.

Chandler 내가 만약 우리 부모처럼 된다면, 스무 살 소년을 따라다니는 술주정뱅이 금발이거나, 아니면 결국 우리 엄마처럼 되겠지.

- a certain point : 특정한 시점
- let go : 놔주다, 어느 정도 포기하다
- even if : ~일지라도, ~한다 하더라도
- a couple of ~ : 몇 개의
- in a couple of years : 몇 년 후에는
- turn into : ~로 변하다
- alcoholic : 형 술에 취한, 명 알코올 중독자
- blond : 형 금발인, 명 금발
- chase after ~ : ~를 다
- end up : 결국 ~하게 되다

61

bail on someone
버리다, 떠나다, 바람맞히다

> **Chandler** Oh, uh, listen, about tonight.
>
> **Chandler** 아, 음, 그거 말이야, 오늘 밤 일.
>
> **Joey** No, no, no, don't you dare <u>**bail on me**</u>. The only <u>reason</u> she's going out with me is because I said I could bring a friend for her friend.
>
> **Joey** 안 돼, 안 돼, 안 돼! 나 버릴 엄두도 내지 마. 그 여자애 나랑 데이트하는 이유가 그녀 친구 위해서 한 명 데리고 간다고 했기 때문이야.

📒 Note

- **bail** : ~를 떠나다. 버리다.

  i.e I'm gonna bail. = 나 떠날(도망갈) 거야.

- **bail on someone / something** : ~로부터 떠나다, ~를 바람맞히다.

  i.e I'm gonna bail on class today. = 땡땡이치다

⏱ Practice

1 너는 나를 버린 걸 후회하게 될 거야.

2 나는 절대 너를 버리지 않을 거야.

3 너 지금 우리 버리는 거야?

4 나는 오늘 요가 수업을 빼먹었어.

주요 장면 STUDY

Rachel Well, what are you guys doing tomorrow night?

Rachel 너희 내일 밤 뭐 하니?

Joey Actually, tomorrow night kinda <u>depends on</u> how tonight goes.

Joey 사실, 내일 밤은 오늘 밤을 어떻게 보내느냐에 따라 달렸지.

Chandler Oh, uh, listen, about tonight.

Chandler 아, 음, 그거 말이야, 오늘 밤 일.

Joey No, no, no, don't you <u>dare</u> **bail on me**. The only <u>reason</u> she's going out with me is because I said I could bring a friend for her friend.

Joey 안 돼, 안 돼, 안 돼! 나 버릴 엄두도 내지 마. 그 여자애 나랑 데이트하는 이유가 그녀 친구 위해서 한 명 데리고 간다고 했기 때문이야.

Chandler Yes, I know, but her friend sounds like such a.

Chandler 그래, 근데 그녀 친구가 약간 좀.

Joey <u>Pathetic</u> <u>mess</u>? I know, but, come on, man, she's <u>needy</u>, she's vulnerable. I'm thinking, <u>cha-ching</u>!

Joey 이상하다고? 그래, 하지만, 그 여자애 자신감이 좀 없고 상처 잘 받아서 그렇지. 내가 보기엔, 돈이 많아.

- depend on ~ : ~에 달리다, ~에 의존하다
- dare : 감히 ~하다 할 엄두를 내다
- bail on someone : ~를 떠나다, 버리다
- reason : 이유
- pathetic : 한심한, 불쌍한, 찌질한

- mess : 엉망진창, 엉망인 상황
- needy : 어려운, 자신감이 없는
- vulnerable : 연약한, 상처받기 쉬운
- cha-ching : 돈 많은(금전 등록기 닫을 때 나는 소리)

set someone up with someone
(이성을) 소개시키다, 엮다

> **Chandler** Calm down? Calm down? You **set me up with** the woman that I've dumped twice in <u>the last</u> five months!
>
> **Chandler** 진정하라고? 진정? 지난 5개월간 내가 두 번이나 찬 여자를 소개팅해주고서?
>
> **Joey** Can you stop <u>yelling</u>? You're making me nervous, and.
>
> **Joey** 소리 좀 그만 지를래? 자꾸 긴장되잖아.

Note

- **set something up** : 설치하다, 세팅하다, 만들다, 일정을 잡다.

- **set A up with someone(B)** : A와 B를 소개시켜주다, 둘 사이를 엮다

- **set A up with something(a job)** : A를 일자리에 소개시키다.

Practice

1 정말 너한테 내 친구 소개시켜주고 싶어.

2 너 지금 나를 그 사람이랑 엮으려는 거야?

3 그녀가 우리를 데이트할 수 있게 엮어줬어요.

4 나는 그녀를 소개시켜달라고 너한테 부탁한 적이 없어.

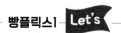
👥 주요 장면 STUDY

Chandler Janice?

Chandler Janice라고?

Janice Oh my God.

Janice 어머나 세 상 에.

Chandler Hey, it's Janice.

Chandler 야, Janice다.

Chandler Ok, I'm <u>making a break for it</u>, I'm going out the window.

Chandler 좋아, 나 달아날 거야. 창문으로 나갈 거야.

Joey No, no, no, don't! I've been waiting for like, forever to go out with Lorraine. Just calm down.

Joey 안 돼. 안 돼. 그러지 마. 나 Lorraine하고 데이트하려고 오랫동안 기다렸다고! 좀 진정해 봐!

Chandler Calm down? Calm down? You **set me up with** the woman that I've dumped twice in <u>the last</u> five months!

Chandler 진정하라고? 진정? 지난 5개월간 내가 두 번이나 찬 여자를 소개팅해주고서?

Joey Can you stop <u>yelling</u>? You're making me nervous, and.

Joey 소리 좀 그만 지를래? 자꾸 긴장되잖아.

- make a break for it : 달아나다, 탈주하다
- set me up with ~ : 나를 누군가와 엮어주다, 나를 소개팅 시켜주다
- the last ~ : 지난 ~
- yell : 고함지르다, 소리치다

It's on me
내가 살게

> **Joey** I'm outta here. Here's my credit card. Dinner's on me. I'm sorry, Chandler.

> **Joey** 지금 갈게. 여기 내 신용카드 있어. 저녁은 내가 살게. 미안해, Chandler.

 Note

- **on me** : 나에게 올리다. 내가 사겠다.

  i.e Dinner's on me. = 내가 저녁 살게.
  Beer's on me. = 내가 맥주 살게.
  It's on the house. - 그냥 공짜로 드리는 거예요.(서비스예요.)
  우리나라에서 흔히 쓰이는 "서비스예요"를 직역한 "It's service" 는 현지에서는 사용하지 않는 표현이다. 그 대신 해당 비용을 식당이 부담한다는 의미의 "It's on the house"를 쓸 수 있다.

Practice

1 먹고 싶은 거 다 시켜! 내가 쏠게.

2 나랑 같이 밥 먹을래? 내가 밥 살게.

3 맥주는 내가 살게.

4 커피는 내가 살게.

5 2차는 제가 살게요, 알았죠?

주요 장면 STUDY

Chandler Ok, you cannot do this to me.

Chandler 좋아, 너 나한테 이러면 안 되지.

Joey You're right, I'm sorry. You're right.

Joey 맞다, 그래 미안. 네가 옳아.

Lorraine Uh, can we have three chocolate <u>mousses</u> to go, please?

Lorraine 음, 우리 초콜릿무스 좀 포장 해주시겠어요?

Joey I'm outta here. Here's my credit card. <u>**Dinner's on me**</u>. I'm sorry, Chandler.

Joey 지금 갈게. 여기 내 신용카드 있어. 저녁은 내가 살게. 미안해, Chandler.

Chandler I hope she <u>throws up</u> on you.

Chandler 저 여자애가 너한테 구토나 했으면 좋겠네.

• mousses : 무스, 크림
• be on me : 내가 살게
• throw up : 구토하다

67

go for

~를 하다, 시도하다, 선택하다

> Janice   I will **go for** that drink.
>
> Janice   술로 할게.
>
> Chandler   You got it. Good woman!
>
> Chandler   바로 그거야, 멋진 여자군!

 Note

- **go for something**
  - **1** 선택하다 **2** 시도해보다(가벼운 '시도'의 개념에 가까움 - 선택하더라도 '~를 먹어볼게' 같은 뉘앙스)

- **go for it** = 한번 해봐, 시도해봐(격려)(=try it)

["go to" vs. "go for"]

> » go to = ~ 방향으로, ~의 장소로 가다(go to school, go to the gym, *go to work)
> » go for = ~의 행동을 해보다(go for a drive, go for a walk, go for a drink)

ㅋ

Practice

1 아이스카페라테 마실 게.

2 너 나랑 같이 산책 나갈래?

3 내가 생각해봤는데, 결국하기로 결정했어.

4 나는 네가 할 수 있을 것 같아. 시도해봐!

👥 주요 장면 STUDY

Janice So, do we have the best friends <u>or what</u>?

Janice 우리 둘 다 베스트 친군가 뭔가 한번 잘 됐지?

Chandler Joey's not a friend. He's a stupid man who left us his credit card. Another drink? Some dessert? A big screen TV?

Chandler Joey는 친구도 아니야. 걔는 신용카드도 우리에게 맡기고 가는 멍청한 녀석이지. 한 잔 더 마실까? 디저트? 아니면 큰 스크린 TV 사줄까?

Janice I will **go for** that drink.

Janice 술도 힐게.

Chandler <u>You got it</u>. Good woman!

Chandler 바로 그거야, 멋진 여자군!

- or what : 인가 뭔가
- go for : ~를 시도하다, 선택하다
- you got it : 그렇고 말고, 바로 그거야

happened to

우연히 ~하게 되다

> **Janice** This is so much fun. This is like a <u>reunion</u> in the <u>hall</u>!
>
> **Janice** 너무 즐겁다. 복도에서의 재회네!
>
> **Monica** Oh, hi, Ross. Yeah. There's someone I want you to say hi to. **He just happened to call.**
>
> **Monica** 응, Ross, 안부 인사할 친구가 있어. 그냥 우연히 전화 온 거야.

Note

- **happen** : 발생하다
- **happened to V** = 우연히 ~하게 되다
- **happened to be V** = 우연히 ~한 상태에 있게 되다
- **just happen to V** : (의도가 없음을 조금 더 강조) 그냥 우연하게도 ~를 하게 되다

Practice

1. 네가 정말 절묘한 순간에 전화를 했어.

2. 제가 우연히 당신이 우는 모습을 봤어요.

3. 내가 우연히 너의 문자를 보게 됐어.

4. 당신이 전화한 그 순간에만 마침 제가 자리에 없었을 뿐이에요.

🎧 주요 장면 STUDY

| Monica | Hey, Janice. |

Monica 어머나, Janice.

Janice Hi, Monica.

Janice 안녕 Monica.

Chandler Ok, well, this was very special.

Chandler 좋아, 아주 특별한 경우였어.

Monica Rach, come see who's out here!

Monica Rachel, 누가 있는지 와서 좀 봐.

Rachel Oh my god. Janice, hi!

Rachel 어머나, Janice. 잘 지냈어?

Chandler Janice is gonna go away now.

Chandler Janice는 막 가려던 참이었어.

Monica I'll be right back.

Monica 금방 올게.

Rachel Oh, Joey, look who it is.

Rachel 오, Joey, 누군지 좀 봐.

Joey Whoa.

Joey 헐.

Chandler Oh, good, Joey's home now.

Chandler 그래, 이제야 Joey가 집에 왔네.

Janice This is so much fun. This is like a <u>reunion</u> in the <u>hall</u>!

Janice 너무 즐겁다. 복도에서의 재회네!

Monica Oh, hi, Ross. Yeah. There's someone I want you to say hi to. \
He just happened to call.

Monica 응, Ross, 안부 인사할 친구가 있어. 그냥 우연히 전화 온 거야.

• reunion : 재결합, 재회

• hall : 복도

• happened to ~ : 우연히 ~하게 되다

71

in the first place

애초에

> **Phoebe** All right. Now we need the <u>semen</u> of a <u>righteous</u> man.
>
> **Phoebe** 좋아, 이제 올바른 남자의 정액이 필요해.
>
> **Rachel** Ok, Pheebs, you know what, if we had that, we wouldn't be doing the ritual **in the first place**.
>
> **Rachel** 근데, Phoebe, 그거 알아? 우리가 그게 있었다면, 애초부터 이런 의식을 안 했겠지?

📝 Note

• **in the first place** = 가장 첫 번째 장소, 즉, 모든 사건의 첫 지점에

❶ 애당초, 애초에(문장 끝에 올 때)

❷ 먼저, 첫째로, 가장 중요하게(문장 앞에 올 때)

⏱ Practice

❶ 애초에 시작하지를 말았어야 했어.

❷ 애초에 너한테 말을 하지 말았어야 했어.

❸ 나는 애초에 네가 왜 이 직업을 선택했는지 이해가 안 돼.

❹ 첫째로, 이건 너랑 상관없는 일이야.

주요 장면 STUDY

Phoebe All right. Now we need the <u>semen</u> of a <u>righteous</u> man.

Phoebe 좋아, 이제 올바른 남자의 정액이 필요해.

Rachel Ok, Pheebs, you know what, if we had that, we wouldn't be doing the ritual **in the first place**.

Rachel 근데, Phoebe, 그거 알아? 우리가 그게 있었다면, 애초부터 이런 의식을 안 했겠지?

Monica Can we just start throwing things in?

Monica 그냥 이것저것 던져 넣는 거로 시작할까?

Phoebe Ok, yeah, ok. Oh, OK.

Phoebe 좋아, 그래. 좋아.

Rachel Ok, Barry's letters. Adam Ritter's <u>boxer shorts</u>.

Rachel 좋아, Barry의 편지, Adam Ritter의 사각 팬티.

Phoebe Ok, and I have the, uh receipt for my dinner with Nokululu Oon Ah Ah.

Phoebe 좋아, 그리고 나는 누쿠눌루 온 아아랑 저녁 먹었던 영수증 넣을래.

- semen : 남자의 정액
- righteous : 올바른, 옳은
- the ritual : 의식 절차, 의식
- in the first place : 애초에, 처음부터
- boxer shorts : 사각 팬티

get on with one's life
(원래 방식대로) 자기 삶을 살아가다

> **Ross** No, it's just, you know the whole "**getting on with your life**" thing. Well, do I have to? I mean, I'm sitting here with this cute woman, and, and, and she's perfectly nice, and, but that there's, that's it.

> **Ross** 아니, 그냥, 뭐 '본인 인생이나 살아라.' 그런 말 알지? 근데 꼭 그래야 해? 여기 방금 귀엽고 완벽하게 멋진 여자를 옆에 두고 있었는데. 근데, 없잖아.

 Note

• **get on with** = ~를 진행해나가다

i.e get on with one's work / one's job / one's business / one's life
  ≫ 자신의 일 / 직업 / 사업 / 삶을 이어나가다.

Practice

1 이제는 너의 삶을 다시 살 때야.

2 나 천천히 내 삶을 회복하고 있어.

3 그녀가 다시 자신의 삶을 되찾는 거 같아서 기뻐.

4 도대체 언제 너는 다시 너의 삶을 살거니?

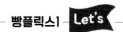

주요 장면 STUDY

Ross   Maybe I <u>screwed up</u> the first date I had in 9 years.

Ross   내가 9년 만에 한 첫 번째 데이트를 망친 거 같네.

Carol   That could be it.

Carol   그런 거 같아.

Ross   Oh, god. You know, this is still pretty hot.

Ross   세상에, 이거 아직도 꽤 뜨거워.

Carol   Mushroom. Smile. They won't all be like this. Some women might even stay <u>through</u> dinner. Sorry, that's not funny.

Carol   버섯이야. 웃어. 여자들이 모두 이렇지는 않을 거야. 저녁 마칠 때까지 있어줄 여자가 생기겠지. 미안해. 별로 안 웃기지.

Ross   No, it's just, you know the whole **"<u>getting on with your life</u>"** thing. Well, do I have to? I mean, I'm sitting here with this cute woman, and, and, and she's perfectly nice, and, but that there's, that's it.

Ross   아니, 그냥, 뭐 '본인 인생이나 살아라.' 그런 말 알지? 근데 꼭 그래야 해? 여기 방금 귀엽고 완벽하게 멋진 여자를 옆에 두고 있었는데. 근데, 없잖아.

- screw up : ~를 망치다
- through ~ : ~내내, ~끝까지
- get on with someone's life : 본인 자신의 인생을 살아가다

at the end of the day

종국에는

Mrs. Tedlock Yes. Well, Mr. Kostelick would like you to <u>stop by</u> his office **at the end of the day**.

Mrs. Tedlock 뭐, 근데, Kostelick 씨가 퇴근 후 사무실로 잠시 들르래요.

Chandler Oh, listen. If this is about those <u>prank</u> memos, I <u>had nothing to do with</u> them. Really. Nothing at all. Really.

Chandler 아, 저기, 장난 메모들 때문이라면, 저는 정말 관계없어요. 전혀요. 진짜예요.

 Note

- **at the end of the day**
  1 날 혹은 하루가 끝나는 시점 / 저녁 퇴근 후
  2 종국에는, 결국에는, 본질적으로

Practice

1 조언은 너무 감사하지만, 결국에는 제가 결정해야 할 일이에요.

2 결국에는 너한테 최선의 선택을 해야 해.

3 결국에는 네가 이긴 사람이 될 거야.

4 결국에는 다 의미 있는 일일 거야.

76

주요 장면 STUDY

Woman Chandler.

Woman Chandler?

Chandler Ms. Tedlock. You're looking lovely today. And may I say, that is a very <u>flattering sleeve length</u> on you.

Chandler Tedlock 씨. 오늘 멋진데요. 제가 그거 돋보이는 소매 길이라고 말해도 되는 거죠?

Mrs. Tedlock Yes. Well, Mr. Kostelick would like you to <u>stop by</u> his office <u>at the end of the day</u>.

Mrs. Tedlock 뭐, 근데, Kostelick 씨가 퇴근 후 사무실로 잠시 들르래요.

Chandler Oh, listen. If this is about those <u>prank</u> memos, I <u>had nothing to do with</u> them. Really. Nothing at all. Really.

Chandler 아, 저기, 장난 메모들 때문이라면, 저는 정말 관계없어요. 전혀요. 진짜예요.

- flattering : 돋보이게 하는, 으쓱하게 하는, 아첨하는, 비위 맞추는
- sleeve length : 소매 길이
- stop by : 잠시 머무르다
- at the end of the day : 하루 끝에, 퇴근 후에, 결국에는
- prank : 농담으로 하는 장난
- have nothing to do with : ~와 전혀 관계가 없다

keep it down

조용히 하다, 목소리를 낮추다

> **Monica** Yeah, well, is that better?
>
> **Monica** 그래, 그래서 더 낫냐고.
>
> **Joey** I don't know. We're talking about whipped fish, Monica. I'm just happy **I'm keeping it down**, you know?
>
> **Joey** 모르겠어. 그냥 거품 난 생선이잖아. Monica. 내가 먹고 있는 것만으로도 기특해.

📓 Note

• **keep it down**

1 조용히 하다.

2 참고 있다.

3 얌전히 있다.

cf keep it up : '소리 볼륨을 높여라'는 뜻 아님 ->(지금 하는 대로) 계속해라

⏱ Practice

1 제발 좀 조용히 해줄래? 나 전화하고 있자나.

2 조용히 좀 해줄래? 나 공부하려고 노력중이야!

3 엄마가 우리 조용히 하래.

4 그 사람 앞에서는 조용히 있는 게 좋을 거 같아.

주요 장면 STUDY

Monica OK, try this salmon mousse.

Monica 좋아, 이 연어 크림 좀 먹어봐.

Joey Mmmm. Good.

Joey 음. 맛있네.

Monica Yeah, Is it better than the other salmon mousse?

Monica 그래. 아까 연어 무스보다 나아?

Joey It's creamier.

Joey 크림이 좀 많아.

Monica Yeah, well, is that better?

Monica 그래, 그래서 더 낫냐고.

Joey I don't know. We're talking about whipped fish, Monica. I'm just happy **I'm keeping it down**, you know?

Joey 모르겠어. 그냥 거품 난 생선이잖아. Monica. 내가 먹고 있는 것만으로도 기특해.

- whipped : 거품 일게 한, 거품 난
- keep it down : 토하지 않다, 토하지 않고 참다

79

take someone by surprise
~를 깜짝 놀라게 하다

> Ross Alright, I __panicked__, alright? **She took me by surprise**. You know, but it wasn't <u>a total loss</u>. I mean, we ended up <u>cuddling</u>.

> Ross 그래, 당황했었단 말이야. 알아? 그녀가 나를 얼마나 놀라게 했는데. 그래도 나쁘지는 않았어. 결국에는 꼭 껴안고 잤거든.

Note

- **surprise someone** : 누구를 놀라게 하다.
- **take someone by surprise** : 예상하지 못한 일로 놀라게 하다. 많이 놀라게 하다.

Practice

1. 솔직히 너의 반응에 내가 좀 놀랐어.

2. 그가 내 일터에 찾아왔을 때 조금 당황했어.

3. 그녀의 발표는 우리 모두를 놀래고 당황하게 했어.

4. 갑자기 내린 비가 우리를 당황하게 했어.

주요 장면 STUDY

Ross Alright, I panicked, alright? **She took me by surprise.** You know, but it wasn't a total loss. I mean, we ended up cuddling.

Ross 그래, 당황했었단 말이야. 알아? 그녀가 나를 얼마나 놀라게 했는데. 그래도 나쁘지는 않았어. 결국에는 꼭 껴안고 잤거든.

Joey Whoaa! You cuddled? How many times?

Joey 와아! 껴안았어? 몇 번이나?

- panic : 겁에 질리다, 겁에 질려 당황하다
- take someone by surprise : ~를 깜짝 놀라게 하다
- total loss : 완전한 손해
- cuddle : 껴안다, 포옹하다

root for

~를 응원하다

> **Joey** You're not going to believe this!
>
> **Joey** 넌 믿지 않겠지만.
>
> **Chandler** It's OK. It's OK. I was always **rooting for** you two kids to <u>get together</u>.
>
> **Chandler** 그래, 좋아. 난 항상 너희 둘이 사귀기를 응원해왔어.

Note

- **root** : 뿌리 / 지지하다, 응원하다.

- **root for someone / something** : 사람 또는 행동이나 결과를 응원하다

Practice

1 너는 어느 팀을 응원해?

2 너는 어떤 후보를 응원해?

3 무슨 일이 있어도 우리는 항상 너를 응원해.

4 저는 항상 당신이 성공하기를 응원해왔어요.

주요 장면 STUDY

Ross I want to take my tongue and.

Ross 내 혀를 가지고.

Ross and.

Ross 그리고.

Joey Say it. say it!

Joey 계속 말해봐. 하라고!

Ross run it all over your body until you're <u>trembling</u> with, with.

Ross 네 온몸을 핥고 싶어. 네가 부르르 떨 때까지.

Chandler with?

Chandler 계속해.

Ross Funny story!

Ross 웃긴 얘기지.

Joey You're not going to believe this!

Joey 넌 믿지 않겠지만.

Chandler It's OK. It's OK. I was always **rooting for** you two kids to <u>get together</u>.

Chandler 그래, 좋아. 난 항상 너희 둘이 사귀기를 응원해왔어.

• tremble : 몸을 떨다, 흔들리다
• root for : ~를 응원하다
• get together : 합치다, 데이트하다

put a roof over someone's head

거처를 마련해주다

> Monica | You know, Rachel, when you ran out of your wedding, I was there for you. I **put a roof over your head**, and if that means nothing to you, twenty dollars an hour.
>
> Monica | 야, Rachel, 너 결혼식에서 도망쳤을 때, 내가 도와줬잖아. 거처까지 마련해줬는데, 그게 너한테는 아무 의미도 아닌 거면, 시간당 20달러는 어때?

📋 Note

• roof = 지붕 / 상징적으로 거처, 집, 안전한 곳

• a roof over one's head = 집 / 거주지(place to live)

• put a roof over someone's head = 살 곳 / 안전하게 거주할 수 있는 곳을 마련해주다.

⏱ Practice

1️⃣ 우리 집이 있다는 게 정말 복받은 거야.

2️⃣ 우리는 부자는 아니지만 적어도 집은 있잖아.

3️⃣ 내 집이 있었으면 좋겠어.

4️⃣ 내가 집을 마련해줬다는 걸 잊지 마.

주요 장면 STUDY

Monica Wendy! Wendy! Wendy!

Monica Wendy! Wendy! Wendy!

Rachel Who was that?

Rachel 누군데?

Monica Wendy <u>bailed</u>. I have no waitress.

Monica Wendy가 약속을 어겼어. 웨이트리스 해줄 사람이 없네.

Rachel Oh, that's too bad. Bye bye.

Rachel 아, 안됐구나. 안녕!

Monica Ten dollars an hour.

Monica 시간당 10달러 줄게.

Rachel No.

Rachel 안 해.

Monica Twelve dollars an hour.

Monica 시간당 12달러.

Rachel Mon. I wish I could, but I've made plans to <u>walk around</u>.

Rachel Monica, 나도 하고 싶지만, 바람 쐬고 오기로 했어.

Monica You know, Rachel, when you ran out of your wedding, I was there for you. I **put a roof over your head**, and if that means nothing to you, twenty dollars an hour.

Monica 야, Rachel, 너 결혼식에서 도망쳤을 때, 내가 도와줬잖아. 거처까지 마련해줬는데, 그게 너한테는 아무 의미도 아닌 거면, 시간당 20달러는 어때?

Rachel Done.

Rachel 좋아.

- bail : 떠나다, 버리다, 약속을 어기다
- walk around : 산책하다, 돌아다니다
- put a roof over someone's head : 거처를 마련해주다

spoil someone's appetite

입맛을 잃게 하다

> **Steve** Ah, cool! <u>Taco shells</u>! You know, these are, they're like a little corn <u>envelope</u>.
>
> **Steve** 와, 죽인다. 타코 쉘이네! 이거요, 꼭 옥수수로 만든 봉투 같이 생겼죠?
>
> **Monica** You know what? <u>You don't want to **spoil your appetite**</u>.
>
> **Monica** 저기요, 이거는 입맛 버려요.

Note

- **spoil someone's appetite** : 입맛을 망치다, 식욕을 잃게 하다.
- **You don't want to** : ~안 하는 게 좋아,

  ie You don't want to go there. : 거기 안 가는 게 좋아.

  You don't want to be late. : 늦지 않는 게 좋아.

  You don't want to spoil your appetite. : 입맛 망치지 않는 게 좋아요. 드시지 마세요.

Practice

1 사탕 주지 마세요. 입맛 버려요!

2 나 안 먹을래. 입맛 잃기 싫어.

3 네가 지금 막 내 입맛을 망쳐놨어.

4 그 영화가 내 입맛을 잃게 했어.

👥 주요 장면 STUDY

Steve Ah, cool! <u>Taco shells</u>! You know, these are, they're like a little corn <u>envelope</u>.

Steve 와, 죽인다. 타코 쉘이네! 이거요, 꼭 옥수수로 만든 봉투 같이 생겼죠?

Monica You know what? <u>You don't want to</u> **spoil your appetite**.

Monica 저기요, 이거는 입맛 버려요.

Steve Hey! <u>Sugar-O's</u>!

Steve 와! 슈가 오 시리얼이다~

Monica You know, if you just wait another six and a half minutes.

Monica 저기, 6분 30초 정도만 기다리시면 돼요.

Steve Macaroni and cheese! We gotta make this!

Steve 마카로니 앤 치즈네! 우리 이거 만들어 먹어요!

- taco shell : 타코 쉘
- envelope : 봉투
- You don't want to ~ : ~하지 않는 게 좋다
- spoil one's appetite : 입맛 버리다
- sugar-O : 시리얼의 일종

cuddle

꼭 껴안다

Joey **You cuddled.**

Joey 껴안기만 했다고.

Ross Yeah, which was nice.

Ross 응, 좋았다니까.

 Note

["hug" vs. "cuddle"]

» hug : 사람을 만났을 때, 인사 치례로 잠깐 껴안다.(일반적인 애정의 포옹)

» cuddle : 애정을 갖고 길게 껴안다.(보통 연인 사이 애정의 포옹)

Practice

1 아무것도 안 할게. 그냥 껴안고 있고 싶어.

2 너네 껴안고 있는 거 봤어.

3 나는 고양이랑 껴안고 있는 시간이 너무 행복해.

4 걔는 아직도 잘 때 껴안고 잘 게 필요해.

주요 장면 STUDY

Joey　Whoa! And the, huh-huh?

Joey　와! 그래서?

Ross　Well, ahem, you know, <u>by the time</u> we'd finished with all the dirty talk, it was kinda late and we were both kind of exhausted, so uh.

Ross　그게 음, 온갖 야한 이야기를 끝냈을 때쯤, 좀 늦었고, 둘 다 지쳐서….

Joey　**You cuddled**.

Joey　껴안기만 했나고.

Ross　Yeah, which was nice.

Ross　응, 좋았다니까.

- by the time : ~할 때까지, ~ 할 때쯤
- cuddle : 꼭 껴안다

89

how come

왜? 어쩌다가?

Joey	No, no. how come you are working here?
Joey	아니, 아니, 어째서 네가 여기서 일하냐고?
Ursula	Right, yeah, cause its close to where I live, and the aprons are really cute.
Ursula	네. 집에서도 가깝고, 앞치마가 예쁘잖아요.

Note

["How come" vs. "why"]

1 Why : 격식적.

How come : 비격식적. 일상적인 표현.

2 Why : 왜? / 격식적. 조금 더 쎈 표현.

How come : 왜? 어째서? 어쩌다가? / 비격식적. 조금 더 부드러운 표현.

i.e Why are you late? : 왜 늦었어? 추궁하는 듯한 표현.

How come you are late? : 왜 어쩌다 늦은 거야? 좀 부드러운 표현.

3 순서 : Why + V + S : Why are you late?

순서 : How come + S + V : How come you are late?

Practice

1 너 왜(어째서) 안 와?

2 너 왜(어째서) 나한테 전화 안 해?

3 너 왜(어째서) 밥 안 먹어?

4 그녀는 오늘 왜(어쩌다가) 수업에 오지 않았어?

👥주요 장면 STUDY

| Joey | There's the waitress. Excuse me, Miss. Hello, Miss? |

| Joey | 저기 직원 있다. 여기요! 여기요? |

| Chandler | It's Phoebe! Hi! |

| Chandler | Phoebe인데? 안녕! |

| Ursula | Hi. Okay, <u>will that be all</u>? |

| Ursula | 안녕하세요. 더 주문하실 거 없나요? |

| Chandler | Wait, wait! What are you doing here? |

| Chandler | 잠깐만, 잠깐. 근데 여기서 뭐 하는 거야? |

| Ursula | Yeah, um, I was over there, and then you said, "Excuse me, hello Miss," so now I'm here. |

| Ursula | 네. 저기 있었다가, "여기요" 해서 여기 지금 온 건데요. |

| Joey | No, no. **How come** you are working here? |

| Joey | 아니, 아니, 어째서 네가 여기서 일하냐고? |

| Ursula | Right, yeah, cause its close to where I live, and the <u>aprons</u> are really cute. |

| Ursula | 네. 집에서도 가깝고, 앞치마가 예쁘잖아요. |

- Will that be all? : 그게 다 인가요? 더 주문하실 거 없나요?
- how come : 왜, 어째서
- apron : 앞치마

in a row

연속으로, 연달아서

> **Ross** And then, **<u>like three days in a row</u>**, he got to the newspaper before I did, and peed all over the crossword.
>
> **Ross** 그러고서는 3일 연속으로, 나보다 먼저 아침 신문지로 가서는 크로스워드 퍼즐에 오줌을 싸놓는 거야.
>
> **Rachel** I've never done that.
>
> **Rachel** 그건 안 해봤네.

Note

- **row** : 줄
- **sit in a row** : 한 줄로 앉다.
- **walk in a row** : 한 줄로 걷다.
- **do something in a row** : 연달아 무언가를 하다.

Practice

▌1 그는 5 경기를 연달아 이겼어.

▌2 그는 3일 연속으로 회사에 안 나왔어.

▌3 나 오늘 시험 / 미팅 3개 연속으로 있어.

▌4 나는 김치찌개를 7일 연속 먹을 수 있어.

주요 장면 STUDY

> **Ross** I don't know whether he's testing me, or just <u>acting out</u>, but my monkey is <u>out of control</u>. But, he keeps erasing the messages on my machine, "<u>supposedly</u>" <u>by accident</u>.

> **Ross** 걔가 나를 테스트 하는 건지 아닌지 모르겠어. 아니면 그냥 행동하는 건지. 아무튼 내 원숭이는 통제 불능이라고. 응답기 메시지를 계속 지우는 거야. 물론, 아마 우연 이겠지만.

> **Rachel** No, yeah, I've done that.

> **Rachel** 아니야, 나도 그거 해봤어.

> **Ross** And then, **like three days in a row**, he got to the newspaper before I did, and peed all over the crossword.

> **Ross** 그러고서는 3일 연속으로, 나보다 먼저 아침 신문지로 가서는 크로스워드 퍼즐에 오줌을 싸놓는 거야.

> **Rachel** I've never done that.

> **Rachel** 그건 안 해봤네.

• act out : 행동을 취하다, 실현하다
• out of control : 통제 불능
• supposedly : 아마도, 추정하건대
• by accident : 우연히
• in a row : 연속으로, 연달아서
• pee : 오줌을 싸다
• crossword : 십자말풀이

catch someone
따라잡다, 만나다

> `Ross` Oh, Pheebs, I'm sorry, I've got to go. I've got <u>Lamaze class</u>.
>
> `Ross` 아, Phoebe 미안한데, 가야겠다. 무통 분만 수업 있거든.
>
> `Chandler` Oh, and I've got Earth Science, but **I'll catch you** in Gym.
>
> `Chandler` 아, 나도 지구 과학 시간 있긴 한데, 그래도 체육관에서 만나.

Note

- **catch** : 잡다, 붙잡다(**Ex.** I caught you : 너를 잡았다 - 잡았다, 요놈!)

- **catch up with ~** :
  - **1** 물리적, 거리적으로 먼저 간 사람을 따라잡다.
  - **2** 진도나 정도, 수준이 앞선 것을 따라잡다.
  - **3** 보충하다, 밀린 이야기를 하다.(**catch up with someone**)

Practice

1 나 아직 일이 좀 남아서 집에서 만나.

2 먼저 가. 뒤따라갈게.

3 나 가야 돼. 나중에 보자.

4 6시 이후에는 사무실에서 나를 볼 수 없을 거예요.

주요 장면 STUDY

Phoebe Oh, oh, she was the first one to <u>start walking</u>, even though I did it later that same day. But, to my parents, by then it was like "yeah, right, well <u>what else</u> is new?"

Phoebe 아, 언니가 걸음마를 먼저 했어. 내가 같은 날 조금 있다가 하긴 했지만. 근데 부모님 한테는, "그래 잘했는데 글쎄 넌 더 새로운 거 없니?" 이런 반응이었지.

Ross Oh, Pheebs, I'm sorry, I've got to go. I've got <u>Lamaze class</u>.

Ross 아, Phoebe 미안한데, 가야겠다. 무통 분만 수업 있거든.

Chandler Oh, and I've got Earth Science, but **I'll catch you** in Gym.

Chandler 아, 나도 지구 과학 시간 있긴 한데, 그래도 체육관에서 만나.

Rachel So, is this just gonna be you and Carol?

Rachel 그래서, Carol하고 둘이 가?

Ross No, Susan's gonna be there, too. We've got dads, we've got lesbians, the whole <u>parenting</u> team.

Ross 아니, Susan도 있을 거야. 아빠에, 레즈비언에, 막강 육아 군단이지.

- start walking : 걸음마를 시작하다
- what else : 그 밖의 다른 거
- Lamaze class : 자연 무통 분만법 수업, 라마즈법
- catch you : 만나다, 따라잡다
- parenting : 육아

grow apart

(크면서) 사이가 멀어지다

> **Phoebe** Well, I mean, I'm not my sister's, you know, whatever, and um, I mean, it's true, we were one <u>egg</u>, once, but uhm, you know, **we've grown apart**, so, um, I don't know, why not? Okay.

> **Phoebe** 글쎄, 난 언니가 아니라서. 아무튼, 그래, 한때는 우리 하나의 난자였어. 하지만, 뭐, 크면서 사이가 멀어졌으니. 모르겠어. 뭐 어때? 그렇게 해.

📔 Note

- **apart** : 떨어져서, 따로

  i.e sit apart from each other. 따로 앉다

- **grow apart** : 크면서 멀어지다. 시간이 지남에 따라 사이가 멀어지다.

⏱ Practice

1 우리는 크면서 자연스럽게 멀어졌어.

2 내가 이사 가고 나서 멀어지게 됐어.

3 어린 시절 친구들은 결국 멀어지게 돼.

4 걱정 마. 우리는 절대 멀어지지 않을 거야.

주요 장면 STUDY

| Joey | Pheebs? |

| Joey | Phoebe? |

| Phoebe | Yeah? |

| Phoebe | 응? |

| Joey | You think it would be okay if I asked out your sister? |

| Joey | 내가 너희 언니한테 데이트 신청해도 괜찮을까? |

| Phoebe | Why? Why would you wanna do that? Why? |

| Phoebe | 왜? 왜 꼭 그러고 싶은데, 왜? |

| Joey | So that if we went out on a date, she'd be there. |

| Joey | 데이트 신청을 해야 너희 언니가 데이트에 나오지. |

| Phoebe | Well, I mean, I'm not my sister's, you know, whatever, and um, I mean, it's true, we were one egg, once, but uhm, you know, **we've grown apart**, so, um, I don't know, why not? Okay. |

| Phoebe | 글쎄, 난 언니가 아니라서. 아무튼, 그래, 한때는 우리 하나의 난자였어. 하지만, 뭐, 크면서 사이가 멀어졌으니. 모르겠어. 뭐 어때? 그렇게 해. |

| Joey | Cool, thanks. |

| Joey | 고마워. |

• ask out : 사귀다
• egg : 달걀, 난자
• grow apart :(시간이 지나면서, 점점) 사이가 멀어지다

miss out(on ~)

(중요한 것을) 놓치다

> **Susan** Look, I don't see why I should have to **miss out** on the coaching training just because I'm a woman.

> **Susan** 있잖아요. 내가 여자라는 이유만으로 왜 코칭 트레이닝 같은 좋은 기회를 놓쳐야 하는지 모르겠어요.

> **Ross** I see. So what do you <u>propose</u> to do?

> **Ross** 그래요, 그럼 어떻게 할까요?

📑 Note

- **miss**

  1 그리워하다, 보고 싶어 하다.

  2 놓치다, 빠지다, 못 보고 지나치다.

  i.e I missed class today. : 나 오늘 수업 빠졌어.

    I missed it. : 못 보고 지나쳤어.

- **miss out(on ~)** : 보통 좋은 기회를 놓치다.('손해본다'는 뉘앙스)

⏰ Practice

1 이거 진짜 좋은 기회야. 놓치지 마.

2 이번 주 파티 빠지지 마.

3 나 그를 볼 기회를 놓쳐서 슬퍼.

4 다음 수업 놓치지 않는 게 좋을 거예요.

주요 장면 STUDY

Ross and Susan What? What? What?

Ross and Susan 뭐가요, 왜?

Susan I am supposed to be the mommy?

Susan 내가 엄마가 돼야 한다고요?

Ross Okay, I'm gonna play my <u>sperm</u> card one more time.

Ross 그래요, 나는 한번 더 정자 카드를 쓸 거예요.

Susan Look, I don't see why I should have to **miss out** on the coaching training just because I'm a woman.

Susan 있잖아요. 내가 여자라는 이유만으로 왜 코칭 트레이닝 같은 좋은 기회를 놓쳐야 하는지 모르겠어요.

Ross I see. So what do you <u>propose</u> to do?

Ross 그래요, 그럼 어떻게 할까요?

Susan <u>I will flip you for it.</u>

Susan 제가 동전을 던져서 결정할게요.

Ross Flip me for it? No, no, no. <u>heads</u>, heads, heads!

Ross 당신이 결정한다고? 아니, 아니, 아니. 앞면! 앞면! 앞면!

Susan On your back, Mom.

Susan 등 대고 누워요. 엄마.

- sperm : 정자
- miss out : 좋은 기회를 놓치다, 중요한 것을 놓치다
- propose : 제안하다, 의도하다
- flip : 휙 뒤집다
- flip for ~: ~를 결정하기 위해 동전을 던지다
- heads : 동전의 겉면

lay off

해고하다, 그만두다

Mr. Douglas Well, we're gonna be **laying off** people in every department.

Mr. Douglas 글쎄, 부서마다 직원을 감원해야겠어.

Chandler Hey, listen, I know I came in late last week, but I slept funny, and my hair was very, very.

Chandler 저기, 있죠, 저 지난주에 지각한 거 아는데요, 제가 그날 잠을 제대로 못 자서요, 제 머리가 굉장히, 굉장히.

Note

["fire" vs. "lay off"]

» fire : 해고당한 사람에게 귀책사유가 있다.

» lay off : 회사 차원의 문제가 있다.

» ~를 그만두다, 끊다의 의미도 있음(stop doing something)

　　i.e You have to lay off smoking.

　　　　You have to lay off drinking.

Practice

1️⃣ 나 정리해고당했어.

2️⃣ 그 해고는 네 잘못이 아니야.

3️⃣ 그 회사는 직원의 10%를 해고하려고 해.

4️⃣ 나 오늘 많은 사람들을 해고해야 했어.

👥 주요 장면 STUDY

Chandler Mr. D, how's it going, sir?

Chandler Douglas 씨, 안녕하세요.

Mr. Douglas Oh, it's been better. The <u>Annual</u> <u>Net Usage</u> <u>Statistics</u> are in.

Mr. Douglas 아, 괜찮아졌네. 그리고 연간 전산망 통계가 나왔어.

Chandler And?

Chandler 그런데요?

Mr. Douglas It's pretty ugly. We haven't seen an <u>ANUS</u> this bad since the seventies.

Mr. Douglas 엉망이야. 70년대 이후 ANUS가 최악이야.

Chandler So what does this mean?

Chandler 무슨 의미죠?

Mr. Douglas Well, we're gonna be **laying off** people in every department.

Mr. Douglas 글쎄, 부서마다 직원을 감원해야겠어.

Chandler Hey, listen, I know I came in late last week, but I <u>slept funny</u>, and my hair was very, very.

Chandler 저기, 있죠, 저 지난주에 지각한 거 아는데요, 제가 그날 잠을 제대로 못 자서요, 제 머리가 굉장히 굉장히.

Mr. Douglas Not you. Relax.

Mr. Douglas 자네 말고. 안심해.

- annual : 연간
- net usage : 전산망 사용
- statistics : 통계
- anus : 항문

- lay off : 정리해고하다, 감원하다
- department : 부서
- sleep funny : 자세를 잘 못 잡아 잠을 못 자다

now that

이제 ~하게 되었으니, ~하니까

Chandler | I'm just trying to find the right moment, you know?

Chandler | 그냥 적당한 순간을 보고 있는 거야.

Rachel | Oh, well, that shouldn't be so hard, **now that you're dating**. "Sweetheart, you're fired, but how about a quickie before I go to work?"

Rachel | 아, 이제 데이트하게 되었으니 어렵지는 않겠네. "자기야, 자기 잘렸어. 나 출근하기 전에 빨리 할까?"

Note

• **now** : 현재, 지금

• **now that** : 이전까지는 그렇지 않았는데 이제 와서 변화가 생겼을 때

　　　　　　　 이제부터는 ~하다 / 이제는 내가 ~하게 되었으니까 ~하다.

Practice

▣ 이제 내가 일 하니까 너 밥 사줄 수 있어.

▣ 이제 비가 그쳤으니까 우리 집에 걸어갈 수 있어.

▣ 이제 시험이 다 끝났으니까 나는 마음껏 잘 수 있어!

▣ 내가 이제 생각해보니까, 네가 맞아.

🔖 주요 장면 STUDY

Monica I can't believe you. You still haven't told that girl she doesn't have a job yet?

Monica 믿을 수가 없네. 아직도 그 여자한테 잘렸다는 말을 못 했다고?

Chandler Well, you still haven't <u>taken down</u> the Christmas lights.

Chandler 그러게, 넌 아직도 크리스마스 전구 안 떼었네?

Monica Congratulations, I think you've found the world's <u>thinnest argument</u>.

Monica 축하해. 세상에서 가장 유치한 논쟁 발견한 거.

Chandler I'm just trying to find the right moment, you know?

Chandler 그냥 적당한 순간을 보고 있는 거야.

Rachel Oh, well, that shouldn't be so hard, **now that you're dating**. "Sweetheart, you're fired, but how about <u>a quickie</u> before I go to work?"

Rachel 아, 이제 데이트하게 되었으니 어렵지는 않겠네. "자기야, 자기 잘렸어. 나 출근하기 전에 빨리 할까?"

• take down : 분해하다, 떼어내다
• a thin argument : 설득력 없는 주장, 유치한 논쟁
• now that : 이제 ~하게 되었으니, ~하니까
• a quickie : 빨리 해치우는 것

sit around

빈둥거리다, ~하며 세월을 보내다

> **Mr. Heckles** You're doing it again.
>
> **Mr. Heckles** 또 시작이군.
>
> **Monica** We're not doing anything. We're just **sitting around** talking, quietly.
>
> **Monica** 저희 아무것도 안 했는데요. 그냥 앉아서 잡담만 하고 있었어요. 조용히.

 Note

- **sit around** + 장소 : ~ 주변에 둘러앉다

  i.e sit around the fire / sit around the table

- **sit around** : 앉아만 있다 / 아무것도 안 하고 빈둥대다 / 허송세월 보내다

Practice

■ 나는 그냥 빈둥대는 게 좋아요.

② 우리 이렇게 빈둥거릴 시간이 없어.

③ 나 빈둥대고 있는 거 아니고 생각하고 있는 거야!

④ 이렇게 빈둥댈 거면 그냥 집에 가.

주요 장면 STUDY

Monica Oh. Hi, Mr. Heckles.

Monica Heckles 씨, 안녕하세요?

Mr. Heckles You're doing it again.

Mr. Heckles 또 시작이군.

Monica We're not doing anything. We're just <u>**sitting around**</u> talking, quietly.

Monica 저희 아무것도 안 했는데요. 그냥 앉아서 잡담만 하고 있었어요. 조용히.

Mr. Heckles I can hear you <u>through the ceiling</u>. My cats can't sleep.

Mr. Heckles 천장으로 다 들린다고. 내 고양이가 잠을 못 자잖아.

Rachel You don't even have cats.

Rachel 고양이도 없으시잖아요.

Mr. Heckles I could have cats.

Mr. Heckles 있을 수도 있어.

Monica Goodbye, Mr. Heckles.

Monica 안녕히 가세요.

Rachel We'll try to <u>keep it down</u>.

Rachel 조심할게요.

- sit around : ~하며 시간을 보내다, 빈둥거리다
- through the ceiling : 천장을 통해서
- keep it down : 조용히 하다, 잠자코 있다

occur to someone

~에게 갑자기 생각이 들다

> Ross I'm gonna be a father.
>
> Ross 아버지가 된다고.
>
> Rachel **This is just occurring to you?**
>
> Rachel 그걸 이제 안 거야?

 Note

- **occur** : 발생하다(happen)

- **occur to someone** : ~에게 어떤 느낌, 생각, 감정이 갑자기 떠오르다

Practice

1 문득 나는 아직 젊다는 생각이 들었어.

2 우리한테 시간이 얼마 없다는 생각이 불현듯 들었어.

3 나한테 연락할 생각을 못 해봤어?

4 나는 네가 걱정할 거라는 생각을 미처 못 했어.

👥 주요 장면 STUDY

Ross I'm gonna be a father.

Ross 아버지가 된다고.

Rachel **This is just occurring to you?**

Rachel 그걸 이제 안 거야?

Ross I always knew I was havin' a baby, I just never <u>realized</u> the baby was having me.

Ross 항상 내가 아기를 가지는 걸로만 알았지, 아기가 나를 가지는 쪽은 전혀 생각을 못했거든.

Rachel Oh, you're gonna be great!

Rachel 잘 해낼 거야.

Ross Aw, how can you say that? I can't even get Marcel to stop eating the <u>bath mat</u>. How am I gonna <u>raise</u> a kid?

Ross 그렇게 말하지 마. 나는 마르셀이 욕조 매트 물어뜯는 것도 단속 못 해. 그런데 내가 어떻게 애를 키우겠냐고.

Chandler You know, Ross, some scientists are now saying that, that monkeys and babies are actually different.

Chandler Ross, 있잖아, 원숭이랑 아이들이 실제로는 다르다는 과학자들도 있어.

• occur to someone : ~에게 갑자기 생각이 들다
• realize : 깨닫다
• bath mat : 욕조 매트
• raise : 키우다

107

get a raise

월급이 오르다

> Chandler Ah, well, maybe that's, ah, because **you're getting a big raise.**
>
> Chandler 글쎄, 아마 당신이 월급이 왕창 오를 거라서 그럴 거야.
>
> Nina I am?
>
> Nina 제가요?

Note

- **raise** : 올라가는 것, 상승
- **get** : 받다
- **get a raise** : 급여가 오르다
  - ⓕ get promoted : 승진하다

Practice

1. 월급 좀 올랐으면 좋겠다.

2. 저는 올해 급여가 오르는 줄 알았는데요.

3. 이제 내 급여가 오를 때가 된 것 같은데.

4. 이번 달부터 급여가 오를 거예요.

주요 장면 STUDY

Nina	Do you have a sec?
Nina	시간 좀 있어요?
Chandler	Ah, sure, Nina. What's up?
Chandler	그럼, Nina, 무슨 일이야?
Nina	I don't know. <u>For the past</u> couple days, people have been avoiding me and giving me these really strange looks.
Nina	모르겠어요. 지난 며칠간, 직원들이 저를 피하고 진짜 이상하게 봐요.
Chandler	Oh, well, ah, maybe that's because they're ah, <u>jealous</u>, of us.
Chandler	이, 그건 이미 사람들이 우리를 질투해서 그러는 걸 거야.
Nina	Maybe. But that doesn't explain why they keep taking my scissors.
Nina	그래요. 근데 가위는 왜 계속 뺏어갈까요?
Chandler	Ah, well, maybe that's, ah, because **you're getting a big raise**.
Chandler	글쎄, 아마 당신이 월급이 왕창 오를 거라서 그럴 거야.
Nina	I am?
Nina	제가요?
Chandler	Sure, why not?
Chandler	그럼, 당연하지.
Nina	Oh my god! You're amazing!
Nina	아 세상에! 너무 멋져요.

- for the past ~ : 지난 ~동안
- jealous : 질투하는, 시기하는
- scissors : 가위
- get a raise : 월급이 오르다

might as well

~하는 게 낫다, ~하는 것도 나쁘지 않다

> **Rachel** Well, alright, then, forget it. <u>Might as well</u> just go home. Ow, ow, ow, ow!
>
> **Rachel** 그래, 그럼 집에 가지 뭐. 아야, 아야, 아야!
>
> **Monica** Okay, okay. Come here. I hate this.
>
> **Monica** 그래, 그래. 알았어. 못 살아.

 Note

["should" vs. "might as well"]

» should : ~ 해야 해.

» might as well : 딱히 나은 대안이 없으니 ~하자. / ~나 하지 뭐.

🔢 We should go home. : 집에 가야 해.(집에 가야 할 이유가 있을 때)

We might as well go home. : 집에나 자기 뭐.(별 대안이 없을 때)

Practice

1 그냥 그를 기다리지 뭐.

2 그냥 네가 하고 싶은 거나 해.

3 피할 수 없다면 그냥 즐겨!

4 잃을 것도 없는데 그냥 데이트 신청이나 한번 해봐.

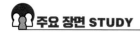

주요 장면 STUDY

Monica You don't have <u>insurance</u>?

Monica 의료보험이 없어?

Rachel Why, how much is this gonna cost?

Rachel 왜, 치료비가 얼마나 나오는데?

Monica I have no idea, but X-rays alone could be a couple hundred dollars.

Monica 모르지, X-ray만 해도 몇 백 달러는 줘야 할걸?

Rachel Well, well, well what are we gonna do?

Rachel 어, 그럼 어떻게 하지?

Monica Well there's not much we can do.

Monica 글쎄, 별로 우리가 할 수 있는 게 없는데.

Rachel Um, unless, unless I use yours.

Rachel 음, 네 걸 쓰는 건 안 돼?

Monica Hah, no, no, no, no, no.

Monica 하, 안 되지, 안 돼.

Rachel Well, now, wait a second, who did I just put as my "<u>In case of emergency</u>" person?

Rachel 잠깐만, 내가 '응급 상황에서 연락할 사람'을 누구를 적었더라?

Monica That's insurance <u>fraud</u>.

Monica 이건 보험 사기야.

Rachel Well, alright, then, forget it. **Might as well** just go home. Ow, ow, ow, ow!

Rachel 그래, 그럼 집에 가지 뭐. 아야, 아야, 아야!

Monica Okay, okay. Come here. I hate this.

Monica 그래, 그래. 알았어. 못 살아.

Rachel Thank you. Thank you. I love you.

Rachel 고마워, 고마워, 사랑해.

- insurance : 보험
- In case of emergency : 응급 상황
- fraud : 사기, 사기꾼
- might as well : ~하는 게 낫다

odds of

~할 가능성

Ross	Tonight.
Ross	오늘 밤.
Joey	Oh, man. **What're the odds of that happening**?
Joey	아, 세상에. 이런 우연이 있나?

📋 Note

- **odd** = 형 이상한, 특이한(**That's odd / She's odd / This place is odd.**)
- **odds** = 명 확률, 가능성(**chance, probability**)
  - » The odds are ~ = ~할 가능성이 있다
  - » The odds of ~ = ~할 확률, ~할 가능성

⏱ Practice

1️⃣ 오늘 비가 올 가능성이 있을 것 같아.

2️⃣ 그가 회복하지 못할 가능성도 있어요.

3️⃣ 여기에서 아는 사람을 만날 확률이 얼마나 돼?

4️⃣ 로또에 당첨될 확률은 굉장히 낮습니다.

👥 주요 장면 STUDY

빵 플 릭 스 1

| Joey | I'm taking Ursula tonight. It's her birthday. |

Joey 오늘 밤 Ursula랑 가려고. 그녀 생일이거든.

Ross Wo-wo-whoa. What about Phoebe's birthday?

Ross 어어, Phoebe 생일은 어쩌고?

Joey When's that?

Joey 언젠데?

Ross Tonight.

Ross 오늘 밤.

Joey Oh, man. **What're the odds of that happening**?

Joey 아, 세상에. 이런 우연이 있나?

• odds of ~ : ~할 가능성
• What are the odds : 이런 우연이 있나, 그럴 확률이 얼마나 되지?

any minute(now)

곧, 당장이라도, 금방이라도

> **Monica** Come on, she'll be here **any minute**.
>
> **Monica** 제발, Phoebe 곧 올 거야.
>
> **Rachel** I hope it's okay.
>
> **Rachel** 괜찮아야 할 텐데.

Note

- **now** : 현재
- **soon** : 현재와 근접한 미래, 곧
- **any minute** : soon 보다 더 급박한 미래.
- **any minute**
  - » any minute now
  - » at any minute
  - » at any minute now

⏱ Practice

1 서둘러, 그들이 곧 올 거야.

2 버스가 당장이라도 올 거야.

3 지금 금방이라도 비가 내릴 것 같아.

4 이 집은 금방이라도 무너질 것 같아 보여요.

👥 주요 장면 STUDY

The Whole Party SURPRISE!

The Whole Party 놀랐지!

Ross What the hell are you doing? You <u>scared</u> <u>the crap outta me</u>.

Ross 뭐 하는 거야! 간 떨어질 뻔했잖아.

Rachel Was that the cake?

Rachel 케익이었어?

Ross Yeah, yeah. I got a lemon <u>smush</u>.

Ross 응, 레몬 곤죽이야.

Monica Come on, she'll be here **any minute**.

Monica 께빈, Phoebe 곧 올 거야.

Rachel I hope it's okay.

Rachel 괜찮아야 할 텐데.

Chandler "Happy Birthday Peehe."

Chandler 생일 축하해 피히.

Monica Well maybe we can make a 'B' out of one of those roses.

Monica 그럼, 저 장미로 'B'를 만들면 되겠네.

Ross Yeah, we'll just use our special cake tools.

Ross 그래, 우리 특별한 케익 툴을 사용하자고.

Phoebe Hey, what's going on?

Phoebe 안녕, 무슨 일 있어?

Ross Oh, we just.

Ross 아, 그냥.

Phoebe's Friends Surprise!

Phoebe's Friends 놀랐지?

Phoebe oh, oh, oh! This is so great! Oh my god!

Phoebe 어머, 어머, 어머! 너무 좋아. 세상에!

• scare : 겁나게 하다
• crap : 쓰레기, 변
• crap out of me : 몸에서(똥이 빠져나간) 간 떨어진

• smush : 곤죽
• any minute : 곧, 당장이라도, 금방이라도

115

be around

근처에 있다, 옆에 있다

Mr. Geller Right, look. Your mother really did the work. I was busy with the business. **I wasn't around that much**. Is that <u>what this is about</u>?

Mr. Geller 그래, 봐봐. 네 엄마가 정말 고생했지. 난 일로 바빴거든. 그렇게 옆에 있어주지 못했단다. 그 일 때문에 따지자는 거야?

Note

- **around** = 대강, 대략, **approximately**, **about**
  - » It's around 2 o'clock.
- **be around** = 거리상으로 가까이 있다, 비유적으로 곁에 있어주다, 옆에 있어주다.

Practice

1 나 한 시간 정도까지는 근처에 있을 거 같아.

2 내일 근처에 계실 건가요?

3 네가 그녀랑 어울리지 말았으면 좋겠어.

4 그는 같이 있으면 너무 재미있어.

주요 장면 STUDY

Ross   Dad, come on, kids!

Ross   아버지, 아기 말이에요!

Mr. Geller   Right, look. Your mother really did the work. I was busy with the business. **I wasn't around that much**. Is that <u>what this is about</u>?

Mr. Geller   그래, 봐봐. 네 엄마가 정말 고생했지. 난 일로 바빴거든. 그렇게 옆에 있어주지 못했단다. 그 일 때문에 따지자는 거야?

• be around : 옆에 있어주다

• what this is about? : 그 일 때문에 그러는 거야?

make up for

만회하다, 화해하다

Mr. Geller 'Cause there's time to **make up for that**. We can do stuff together. You always wanted to go to that <u>Colonial Williams burg</u>. How about we do that?

Mr. Geller 만회할 시간이 있잖니. 지금도 우리 할 수 있단다. 너 항상 Colonial Williams burg 가고 싶어 했잖니. 거기 가볼까?

Note

• **make up**

  명 화장(품)(put on make-up)

  동 만들어내다(make up stories)

  화해하다(we need to make up)

  만회하다(<u>make up for</u> my mistake)

Practice

1 내 잘못을 만회할 수 있는 기회를 주세요.

2 당신은 잘못을 만회할 수 있는 시간이 있어.

3 무슨 수를 써서라도 손실을 메우도록 해.

4 내가 약속 시각에 늦었으니까 밥 살게.

👥 주요 장면 STUDY

| Ross | No, no, Dad, I was just wondering. |

| Ross | 아뇨, 아뇨 아빠, 그냥 궁금해서요. |

| Mr. Geller | 'Cause there's time to **make up for that**. We can do stuff together. You always wanted to go to that <u>Colonial Williamsburg</u>. How about we do that? |

| Mr. Geller | 만회할 시간이 있잖니. 지금도 우리 할 수 있단다. 너 항상 Colonial Williamsburg 가고 싶어 했잖니. 거기 가볼까? |

| Ross | Thanks, Dad, really, I ju, you know, I just, I just needed to know, um, when did you start to feel like a father? |

| Ross | 됐어요. 아빠. 저는 그냥 알고 싶었어요. 아빠가 되었다고 실감하신 게 언제예요? |

• make up for : 만회하다, 화해하다
• Colonial Williamsburg : 버지니아에 위치한 미국의 민속촌

be spoiled

버릇없는, 오냐오냐 큰

> Dr. Mitchell God bless the <u>chickpea</u>.
>
> Dr. Mitchell 병아리콩에게 축복을!
>
> Monica Oh, god, **I am so spoiled.** That's it!
>
> Monica 아, 세상에. 난 정말 싸가지가 없어요. 그렇다고요!

 Note

• spoil : ~를 망치다, 엉망으로 만들다

  spoil the children : 아이를 버릇없게 키우다

• **be spoiled** : 버릇없이 큰, 싸가지가 없는, 오냐오냐 큰

  [주의] 무조건 부정적으로만 쓰이지는 않음 : **You are spoiling me!**(나한테 너무 잘해줄 때)

Practice

1 그 사람 너무 싸가지가 없어서 싫어.

2 나도 내가 싸가지가 없다는 걸 알아요.

3 그 아이들은 벌써부터 아주 버릇이 없어.

4 나는 그날 너무 행복했어.

🐧 주요 장면 STUDY

Monica Yeah, see, I was supposed to get married, but, um, I left the guy at the altar.

Monica 네, 뭐 전 결혼할 뻔했다가, 뭐, 결혼식장에서 신랑 두고 도망쳤어요.

Dr. Mitchell Really?

Dr. Mitchell 정말이요?

Monica Yeah, Yeah, I know it's pretty selfish, but, hey, that's me. Why don't you try the <u>hummus</u>?

Monica 네. 네. 굉장히 이기적인 거 알죠. 근데, 그게 나예요. 후무스 좀 드셔보세요.

Dr. Rosen So, Monica, what do you do?

Dr. Rosen Monica는 직업이 뭐예요?

Rachel Ah, I'm a chef at a restaurant uptown.

Rachel 아, 전 시내 레스토랑 요리사예요.

Dr. Rosen Good for you.

Dr. Rosen 멋지네요.

Rachel Yeah it is, <u>mostly</u> because I get to <u>boss</u> people around, which I just love to do.

Rachel 그렇죠. 주로 직원들 쥐고 흔드는 거 때문에 일하는 게 즐거워요.

Dr. Rosen This hummus is great.

Dr. Rosen 이 후무스 정말 맛있네요.

Dr. Mitchell God bless the <u>chickpea</u>.

Dr. Mitchell 병아리콩에게 축복을!

Monica Oh, god, **I am so spoiled**. That's it!

Monica 아, 세상에. 난 정말 싸가지가 없어요. 그렇다고요!

- altar : 제단, 결혼식장
- hummus : 후무스(병아리콩을 으깨어 만든 중동 요리)
- mostly : 주로, 대개
- boss : 📘 상사

- boss someone around : 📗 ~를 쥐고 흔들다
- chickpea : 병아리콩
- be spoiled : 버릇없이 크다, 싸가지가 없다, 오냐오 나하며 키워지다

121

stand someone up

바람맞히다

Phoebe	Trouble?
Phoebe	문제 있는 거야?
Joey	Your sister **stood me up** the other night.
Joey	네 언니가 지난 밤 나 바람맞혔어.
Phoebe	Oh, no. Don't you hate it when people aren't there for you?
Phoebe	저런, 너 사람들이 바람맞히는 거 싫어하지 않아?

Note

• stand someone up

  = leave someone standing : 서 있는 채로 두다 / 바람맞히다.

Practice

1 아마도 그가 나를 바람맞힌 것 같아.

2 그 날 너를 바람맞혀서 정말 미안해.

3 너 또 그렇게 나를 바람맞힐 거야?

4 아니, 다시는 너를 바람맞히지 않을 거야.

👥 주요 장면 STUDY

Joey	Hey.
Joey	안녕
Ross and Chandler	Hey!
Ross and Chandler	안녕
Monica	Hi.
Monica	안녕
Chandler	She still didn't call?
Chandler	아직 그녀한테 전화 안 와?
Joey	No.
Joey	응.
Phoebe	Trouble?
Phoebe	문제 있는 거야?
Joey	Your sister **stood me up** the other night.
Joey	네 언니가 지난 밤 나 바람맞혔어.
Phoebe	Oh, no. Don't you hate it when people aren't there for you?
Phoebe	저런, 너 사람들이 바람맞히는 거 싫어하지 않아?
Ross	What is that?
Ross	그건 무슨 단어야?
Monica	Tushy!
Monica	볼기!
Ross	Well, did you try calling her?
Ross	전화는 해봤어?
Joey	I've been trying for two days. When I called the restaurant, they said she was too busy to talk. I can't believe she's blowin' me off.
Joey	이틀 동안 했어. 식당에 전화하니까 바쁘다더라. 이렇게 날 차다니.

• stand someone up : ~를 바람맞히다

157 SCENE

be nuts / nutsy about

굉장히 좋아하다

Phoebe	Does he know?
Phoebe	그 사람도 알아?
Ursula	Who?
Ursula	누구?
Phoebe	Joey. You know, um, **he's really nutsy about you**.
Phoebe	Joey 말이야. 있지, 그 남자 언니 무지 좋아해.

Note

- **nuts** : "미쳤다"는 의미를 가진 비격식적 표현(=**crazy**)

- **nutsy** : **nuts**한 사람, 상태를 표현하는 **slang**.

   i.e You are nuts = You are crazy.

   Are you nuts? = Are you crazy?

   You are driving me nuts. = You are driving me crazy.

- **be nuts / nutsy about something / someone**(~를 무척 / 미치도록 좋아하다)

Practice

① 나는 진짜 스포츠광이야.

② 그 사람은 영화광이야.

③ 그가 나를 굉장히 좋아하는 거 나도 알아.

④ 그가 나를 좋아하든 말든 상관없어.

🗣️ 주요 장면 STUDY

Phoebe	So, <u>what's the deal with</u> umm, you and Joey?
Phoebe	근데, 언니랑 Joey랑은 어떻게 된 거야?
Ursula	Oh, right. He is so great. But that's over.
Ursula	아 맞아, 정말 그 사람 괜찮지. 근데 끝났어.
Phoebe	Does he know?
Phoebe	그 사람도 알아?
Ursula	Who?
Ursula	누구?
Phoebe	Joey. You know, um, **he's really nutsy about you**.
Phoebe	Joey 말이야. 있지, 그 남자 언니 무지 좋아해.
Ursula	He is? Why?
Ursula	그 남자가? 왜?
Phoebe	<u>You got me</u>.
Phoebe	나도 모르지.
Ursula	Right.
Ursula	그래.
Ursula	Excuse me. Doesn't this <u>come with</u> a side salad?
Ursula	죄송한데, 샐러드 같이 나오지 않나요?
Phoebe	So, um, are you gonna call him?
Phoebe	그래서, 전화할 거야?
Ursula	What? Do you think he likes me?
Ursula	왜? 그가 나 좋아하는 거 같아?
Phoebe	No, Joey.
Phoebe	아니, Joey 말이야.
Ursula	Oh. No, no, he is so smart. He'll <u>figure it out</u>.
Ursula	아니, 그는 똑똑해서 눈치 챌 거야.

- what's the deal with ~ : ~와는 무슨 일이야? / ~와는 왜 그래?
- be nutsy about ~ : ~를 굉장히 좋아하다
- You got me : 나도 모르지
- come with ~ : ~와 같이 곁들이다
- figure it out : 찾아내다, 알아내다

125

worst case scenario
최악의 경우에

Chandler Okay, **worst case scenario**. <u>Say</u> you never feel like a father.

Chandler 좋아, 최악의 경우, 네가 아버지라는 걸 못 느낀다고 치자.

Ross Uh-huh.

Ross 응.

 Note

• (the) worst case = 최악의 경우, 상황

• (the) worst case scenario = 최악의 시나리오(스토리, 이야기의 진행)를 생각해보자

• In the ~ / Let's think of ~ / If we think of ~ 으로 쓰는 게 문법상으로 맞지만, 일상 대화에서 그냥 아무것도 없이 Worst case scenario, 이렇게 많이 쓰임.

• 반대 = best case scenario

• Say ~ = ~라고 가정해보자, ~라고 치자.

⏱ Practice

1 최악의 경우에 우리 집에 못 갈지도 몰라.

2 최악에 경우에 모든 걸 잃게 될 수도 있어.

3 우리 최악의 경우를 생각해봐야 할 것 같아.

4 여기서 최악의 경우는 집에 걸어가야 하는 거야.

주요 장면 STUDY

Chandler Okay, **worst case scenario**. Say you never feel like a father.

Chandler 좋아, 최악의 경우, 네가 아버지라는 걸 못 느낀다고 치자.

Ross Uh-huh.

Ross 응.

Chandler Say your son never feels <u>connected to</u> you, as one. Say all of his <u>relationships are affected by</u> this.

Chandler 아들 하고 너 하고 하나라는 교감을 못 느낀다고 쳐봐. 그 아이의 모든 인간관계가 이것 때문에 영향을 받는다고 쳐봐.

Ross Do you have <u>a point</u>?

Ross 요점이 뭔데?

Chandler You know, you think I would.

Chandler 나한테 그런 게 있을까?

- worst case scenario : 최악의 경우에
- Say ~ : ~라고 치자
- connected to ~ : ~에 연결된
- relationship : 둘 이상에서의 관계
- be affected by ~ : ~에게 영향을 받다
- point : 요점, 주제

get over
극복하다, 잊다(~로부터 회복하다)

> Joey | Then, uh, then I'm sorry.
>
> Joey | 그럼, 미안하게 됐어.
>
> Phoebe | You know, You're gonna be really, really hard to **get over**.
>
> Phoebe | 있지, 너를 잊기는 정말 힘들 거야.
>
> Joey | I know.
>
> Joey | 알지.

 Note

• **get over** : ~를 넘어서다 / ~를 극복하다 / 누군가를(그리워하는 마음을) 잊다.

• **be over** : (이미) 다 잊다

Practice

① 나는 그를 잊으려고 노력중이야.

② 나는 그를 다 잊었다고 생각했는데, 아니었나봐.

③ 1년이나 됐는데 아직도 그녀를 못 잊은 거야?

④ 나는 평생 그녀를 못 잊을 것 같아.

주요 장면 STUDY

Joey Oh, Urse.

Joey 오— Ursula!

Phoebe Okay, yeah, so it's not gonna work.

Phoebe 좋아, 이제는 소용없어.

Joey Why? Is it because I'm friends with Phoebe?

Joey 왜? 내가 Phoebe랑 친구여서 그래?

Phoebe If it was, would you stop <u>hanging out with</u> her?

Phoebe 만약 그거라면, Phoebe랑 안 만날 수 있어?

Joey No. no, I, I couldn't do that.

Joey 아니, 아니, 그럴 수는 없지.

Phoebe Um, then yes, it's 'cause of Phoebe! So, you know, it's either her or me.

Phoebe 음, 그러면, Phoebe 때문이야. 그래서, 그녀야 나야.

Joey Then, uh, then I'm sorry.

Joey 그럼, 미안하게 됐어.

Phoebe You know, You're gonna be really, really hard to **get over**.

Phoebe 있지, 너를 잊기는 정말 힘들 거야.

Joey I know.

Joey 알지.

• hang out with ~ : ~와 함께하다
• get over : 극복하다, 잊다

129

run low(on)

~가 모자라다, 고갈되다

> **Ross** Uh, Rach, we're **running low on** <u>resumes</u> over here.
>
> **Ross** 아, Rachel, 여기 네 이력서 다 떨어져간다.
>
> **Monica** Do you really want a job with Popular <u>Mechanics</u>?
>
> **Monica** Popular 정비사에서 일하고 싶어?

 Note

- **run low on** : ~가 결핍, 고갈되다(=**run short**)

  i.e we are running low on water. = we are running short on water.

- **low / high** 완전히 반대되는 뜻 아님. 조금 다르게 쓰임.(**keep down / up**처럼)

- **run high** : ~가 고조되다(보통 감정, 긴장 - **emotions, tensions**)

  i.e The tension between the two is running high.

⏱ Practice

① 우리 차 연료가 좀 부족한 거 같은데?

② 우리 시간이 별로 없어.

③ 그들은 깨끗한 물이 고갈되어 있어.

④ 우리는 곧 자원이 고갈될 거예요.

🗣 주요 장면 STUDY

Ross Uh, Rach, we're **running low on** resumes over here.

Ross 아, Rachel, 여기 네 이력서 다 떨어져간다.

Monica Do you really want a job with Popular Mechanics?

Monica Popular 정비사에서 일하고 싶어?

Chandler Well, if you're gonna work for mechanics, those are the ones to work for.

Chandler 글쎄, 너 거기서 일하면, 그 사람들이 너랑 일하느라 애먹겠다.

- run low on : ~가 모자라다, 고갈되다
- resumes : 이력서
- mechanics : 정비공, 정비회사

for real
진짜로, 진지하게

Chandler OK, so at this point, the dealer···

Chandler 좋아, 여기서 딜러는···

Monica Alright, you know, we got it, we got it. **Let's play for real.**
High stakes. big bucks.

Monica 좋아, 알았어. 이해했어. 진짜로 게임하자. 이판 사판으로, 큰돈 걸고

 Note

["for real" vs. "really"]

» 'really'도 격식적인 표현은 아니지만 'for real'이 조금 더 비격식적인 표현

» 일상에서는 'for real'이 'really'보다 더 자연스러움

» 놀라운 뉴스를 들었을 때 : Really? 보다 For real? 이 더 놀람의 감정을 크게 전달함.

• **do something for real** : ~를 진지하게 하다, 제대로 하다.

📗 Let's play for real. : 정말 제대로 게임하자.

Practice

1️⃣ 너 회사 그만뒀어? 진짜로?

2️⃣ 우리 진지하게 하고 있어.

3️⃣ 너는 하는 척만 하고 있잖아. 진지하게 하고 있지 않아.

4️⃣ 나 이번에는 진짜 제대로 할 거야.

주요 장면 STUDY

Chandler OK, so at this point, the dealer...

Chandler 좋아, 여기서 딜러는...

Monica Alright, you know, we got it, we got it. **Let's play for real.**
High stakes. big bucks.

Monica 좋아, 알았어. 이해했어. 진짜로 게임하자. 이판사판으로, 큰돈 걸고

Ross Alright, now, you sure? Phoebe just threw away two jacks because they didn't look happy.

Ross 좋아, 정말 하고 싶어? Phoebe는 방금 행복해 보이지 않는다고 잭을 두 장이나 버렸어.

• for real : 진지하게, 진짜로
• high stakes : 흥하든 망하든, 이판사판으로.
• big bucks : 큰돈

bluff

허세를 부리다

Joey	**I was bluffing.**
Joey	그냥 뻥카 한 거야.
Phoebe	A-ha! And what is bluffing? Is it not another word for lying?
Phoebe	아하! 뻥카가 뭐야? 거짓말의 다른 표현이야?

📑 Note

- **bluff 동** : 허세를 부리다, 허풍 떨다(**He's just bluffing. Stop bluffing.**)

- **bluff 명** : 허세, 속임수, 허풍

- **bluffing in poker** : 실제 가진 것보다 많은 것을 가진 척하는 것.(뻥카)

- **bluff someone into doing something** : 허세나 속임수로 상대가 어떠한 행동을 하게 하다.

⏱ Practice

1 걱정 마. 저 사람 그냥 다 허세야.

2 너 그거 그냥 다 허세인 거 알아.

3 내가 허세 아니라고 말했잖아요.

4 내가 볼 때 그건 자신감이라기보다는 허세에 가까워요.

🎭 주요 장면 STUDY

Phoebe　Oh I see, so then, you were lying.

Phoebe　좋아, 알겠어, 너 거짓말했지?

Joey　About what?

Joey　뭘?

Phoebe　About how good your cards were.

Phoebe　얼만큼 패가 좋은지 말이야.

Joey　**I was bluffing.**

Joey　그냥 뻥카 한 거야.

Phoebe　A-ha! And what is bluffing? Is it not another word for lying?

Phoebe　아하! 뻥카가 뭐야? 거짓말의 다른 표현이야?

• bluff : 허세를 부리다, 엄포를 놓다

135

owe someone something

갚을 빚이 있다

> Ross The game, Rachel, the game. **You owe us money for the game**.
>
> Ross 게임하자, Rachel, 게임하자고. 게임한다고 우리한테 돈도 빌렸잖아.
>
> Rachel Oh. Right.
>
> Rachel 아, 맞다.

 Note

• **owe** : 빚을 지다, 금전적인 빚을 지다, 채무를 지다.(마땅히 주어야 할 어떤 것)

    i.e I owe you lunch / dinner / coffee. : 내가 점심 / 저녁 / 커피 살게.
    You owe me an apology / an explanation. : 너 나한테 사과 / 설명해야 해.

Practice

1 너 나한테 점심 값 $20 줘야해.

2 내가 너한테 더 갚아야 할 거 있니?

3 영어 가르쳐줬으니 내가 저녁 살게.

4 너 나한테 설명해야 될 거 있는 것 같은데.

주요 장면 STUDY

Ross The game, Rachel, the game. **You owe us money for the game.**

Ross 게임하자, Rachel, 게임하자고. 게임한다고 우리한테 돈도 빌렸잖아.

Rachel Oh. Right.

Rachel 아, 맞다.

Joey You know what, you guys? It's their first time, why don't we just forget about the money, alright?

Joey 얘들아, 얘들은 처음이잖아. 돈은 걸지 말고 쳐.

Monica Hell no, we'll pay!

Monica 싫어, 돈 낼 거야.

Phoebe OK, Monica? I had another answer <u>all-ready</u>.

Phoebe 좋아, Monica, 난 다른 답을 하려고 만발의 준비를 했는데.

• owe someone something : ~에게 갚을 빚이 있다
• all-ready : ~할 준비가 다 된, ~할 생각이 간절한

beg to differ

생각이 다르다

Monica Please! I am not as bad as Ross.

Monica 제발! Ross 오빠만큼은 아니야.

Rachel Oh, **I beg to differ**. The Pictionary incident?

Rachel 아, 과연 그럴까? 그림 단어 게임 사고는?

Note

• **beg**

　❶ 간청하다, 애원하다.(beg money, I beg you = 제발요)

　❷ 예의 차릴 때 쓰임(I beg your pardon? 뭐라고요?)

• **I beg to differ** = 다르기를 간청하다 즉, 외람되지만 / 실례지만, 제 의견은 다릅니다.

　≫ 친구 사이 뉘앙스 = 과연 그럴까? 정말 그래? 확실해?

Practice

❶ 이건 너랑 상관없는 일이야.

　정말 그럴까?

❷ 우리 이 프로젝트를 그만두어야 될 것 같습니다.

　제 의견은 좀 다릅니다.

❸ 나는 그가 세상에서 노래 제일 잘하는 것 같아.

　나는 그렇게 생각하지 않는데?

❹ 그녀는 혼자 할 수 있다고 하지만, 나는 그렇게 생각하지 않아.

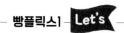

주요 장면 STUDY

Monica Please! I am not as bad as Ross.

Monica 제발! Ross 오빠만큼은 아니야.

Rachel Oh, **I beg to differ**. The <u>Pictionary</u> incident?

Rachel 아, 과연 그럴까? 그림 단어 게임 사고는?

Monica That was not an <u>incident</u>! I was <u>gesturing</u>, and the <u>plate</u> <u>slipped out of my hand</u>.

Monica 그게 무슨 사고야! 그냥 단어 설명하려고 몸짓하다가, 접시가 손에서 미끄러져 깨졌을 뿐인데.

- beg to differ : 의견이 다르다
- I beg to differ. :(친구 사이에) 과연 그럴까?
- pictionary :   그림으로 단어를 알아맞히는 게임
- incident : 특이한, 일, 사건
- gesture : 몸짓을 하다
- plate : 접시
- slip out of my hand : 내 손에서 미끄러지다

SCENE

give something a go

시도해보다

> **Ross** Uh, Rach, do you want me to <u>shuffle</u> those?
>
> **Ross** Rachel, 내가 카드 섞어줄까?
>
> **Rachel** No, no, thats OK. You know, I think **I'm gonna give it a go.**
>
> **Rachel** 아니, 아니, 괜찮아, 내가 한번 해볼게.

Note

- **a go = a try**(한번 해보는 시도, 도전)

- **give it a go = give it a try = give it a shot**(한번 시도해보다.)

- **go for something = try something**(~를 시도해보다.)

Practice

1 한 번도 해본 적 없지만 한번 도전해볼게.

2 할 수 있을지 모르겠지만 도전해볼게.

3 나는 게임을 잘 못하지만 이번에 한번 도전해볼게.

4 시도라도 한번 해 보는 게 어때?

주요 장면 STUDY

Monica Let's play poker.

Monica 포커 게임하자!

Joey Alright now listen, you guys, we talked about it, and if you don't wanna play, we completely understand.

Joey 좋아, 잘 들어. 아까 얘기했지만, 원치 않아도 우리 다 이해해.

Chandler Oh yes, yes, we could play some other game like, uh, I don't know, Pictionary?

Chandler 오 그래, 그래 다른 게임도 괜찮아. 그럼 난이 게임 같은 거?

Monica Ha, ha, very funny, very funny. But I think we'd like to give poker another try. Shall we, ladies?

Monica 하하, 정말 웃기네, 그래도 포커 다시 치고 싶어. 어때 숙녀분들?

Phoebe and Rachel Yes, we should. I think we should.

Phoebe and Rachel 그럼, 당연히 좋지.

Ross Uh, Rach, do you want me to <u>shuffle</u> those?

Ross Rachel, 내가 카드 섞어줄까?

Rachel No, no, thats OK. You know, I think **I'm gonna give it a go**.

Rachel 아니, 아니, 괜찮아, 내가 한번 해볼게.

Rachel Alright.

Rachel 좋아.

• shuffle : 섞다

• give it a go : 시도해보다

141

step on someone's point

다른 사람이 말하는데 끼어들다, 상대의 말을 무시하다

> **Monica** You know what? This is not over. We will play you again, and we will win, and you will lose, and you will beg, and we will laugh, and we will take every last dime you have, and you will hate yourselves forever.
>
> **Monica** 그거 알아? 이게 끝이 아니야. 우린 다시 할 거고, 우리가 이길 거야. 그러면 너희는 질 거고, 구걸하겠지. 그럼 우린 비웃으면서 너희가 가진 동전까지도 다 털 거야. 그럼 너흰 영원히 스스로를 경멸하겠지.
>
> **Rachel** Hmm. **Kinda stepped on my point there**, Mon.
>
> **Rachel** 음, 그렇게 내 요점을 깔아뭉개면 어떡해? Monica.

📖 Note

- **step on something** : ~을 밟다
  - **i.e** You stepped on my toe. : 제 발을 밟으셨어요.
- **step on someone's point** : 상대의 주장을 밟다, 끼어들다, 무력화시키다.
  - **i.e** You stepped on my point. : 내 말에 네가 끼어들었어.(내 말을 네가 끊었어)

⏱ Practice

1 내 말 좀 가로막지 말아줄래?

2 내가 이야기를 끝내려고 했는데 그녀가 자꾸 끼어들었어.

3 상대방의 의견을 가로막는 건 무례한 일이에요.

4 나는 상대의 의견을 가로막는 걸 좋아하지 않아요.

주요 장면 STUDY

Rachel Mm-hmm. Oh, so <u>typical</u>. Ooo, I'm a man. Ooo, I have a peanuts. (-> Ooo, I have a penis.) Ooo, I have to win money to <u>exert</u> my power over women.

Rachel 흠, 너무 전형적이야. 아, 나 남자거든, 아 난 사나이야. 아 난 여자에게 힘을 행사하기 위해 돈을 따야 해.

Monica You know what? This is not over. We will play you again, and we will win, and you will lose, and you will beg, and we will laugh, and we will take every last dime you have, and you will hate yourselves forever.

Monica 그거 일아? 이게 끝이 아니야. 우린 다시 힐 거고, 우리가 이길 기아. 그리면 니희는 질 거고, 구걸하겠지. 그럼 우린 비웃으면서 너희가 가진 동전까지도 다 털 거야. 그럼 너흰 영원히 스스로를 경멸하겠지.

Rachel Hmm. **Kinda stepped on my point there**, Mon.

Rachel 음, 그렇게 내 요점을 깔아뭉개면 어떡해? Monica.

- typical : 전형적인
- exert :(힘, 권력을) 행사하다
- step on : 끼어들다 짓밟다
- step on my point : 내 말에 끼어들다, 내 말을 무시하다

143

be full of it

허풍 떨다, 말이 안 되는 소리를 하다

> **Rachel** What do you mean, you fold? Hey, come on! What is this?
> I thought that 'once the cards <u>were dealt</u>, I'm not a nice guy.'
> I mean, what, **were you just full of it**?
>
> **Rachel** 뭐야, 빠지다니. 이러지 마! 이게 뭐야? 일단 카드를 돌리면, 친구고 뭐고 없다며.
> 다 허풍이었어?

📋 Note

- **bluff** : 허세 부리는 목적성이 뚜렷한 표현.

- **be full of something** : ~가 가득하다

- **be full of it** = it는 보통 가치 없고, 의미 없고, 신뢰가 가지 않는 것으로 해석

  (crap, bullshit, lies)

⏱ Practice

1️⃣ 나는 허세 부리는 사람들을 별로 좋아하지 않아.

2️⃣ 그녀의 말을 믿는 거야? 완전히 허세야!

3️⃣ 그는 본인이 백만장자라고 하는데 그냥 허세인 것 같아.

4️⃣ 솔직히 말하면, 전 당신이 다 허세인 줄 알았어요.

주요 장면 STUDY

Rachel Loser?

Rachel 패배자님은?

Ross No, I fold.

Ross 아니, 나 빠질래.

Rachel What do you mean, you fold? Hey, come on! What is this? I thought that 'once the cards <u>were dealt</u>, I'm not a nice guy.' I mean, what, **were you just full of it**?

Rachel 뭐야, 빠지다니. 이러지 마! 이게 뭐야? 일단 카드를 돌리면, 친구고 뭐고 없다며. 나 허풍이었어?

• fold : 접다
• be dealt : 다루어지다
• be full of it : 허풍 떨다, 말이 안 되는 소리를 하다

145

be in disbelief
믿을 수가 없다

Chandler You know, I can't believe we are even having this discussion.

Chandler 우리가 이런 대화를 할 줄은 상상도 못 했어.

Joey I agree. **I'm, like, in disbelief.**

Joey 맞아. 나도 믿기지가 않아.

📑 Note

• **I'm in disbelief.** : 나는 믿고 싶지 않아. 믿을 수가 없어. 현실회피(**I reject to believe it.**)

⏱ Practice

1 그녀는 나를 정말 믿을 수 없다는 표정으로 바라봤어.

2 우리는 서로를 믿을 수 없다는 표정으로 쳐다봤어.

3 네가 믿을 수 없다는 거 이해해.

4 나는 믿을 수가 없어서 그냥 고개를 절레절레 저었어.

주요 장면 STUDY

Chandler You know, I can't believe we are even having this discussion.

Chandler 우리가 이런 대화를 할 줄은 상상도 못 했어.

Joey I agree. **I'm, like, in disbelief.**

Joey 맞아. 나도 믿기지가 않아.

Chandler I mean, don't you think if things were gonna happen with Rachel, they would've happened already?

Chandler 내 말은, Rachel 하고 일이 생길 거였으면, 벌써 일어나지 않았을까?

Ross **I'm telling you,** she said she's looking for a <u>relationship</u> with someone <u>exactly</u> like me.

Ross 진짜라니까, 딱 나 같은 사람과 사귀고 싶다고 얘기했다니까.

Joey She really said that?

Joey 정말 그렇게 말했어?

Ross Well, I added the 'exactly like me' part.

Ross 뭐, '딱 나 같은' 부분은 좀 덧붙인 거지만.

- be in disbelief : 믿을 수가 없다
- I'm telling you : 진짜라니까
- relationship : 관계
- exactly : 틀림없이, 확실히

go with

어울리다

> **Monica** Which ones?
>
> **Monica** 어떤 신발이냐고.
>
> **Rachel** Oh. Oh, those little <u>clunky</u> <u>Amish</u> things you think **go with** everything.
>
> **Rachel** 아, 아, 너 좋다고 아무 옷에나 신고 다니는 그 작고 투박한 신발 있잖아.

📋 Note

- **go with** : 같이 가다, 어울리다.

- **o well with, go great with** :(음식, 옷, 색깔 등) 잘 어울리다.

- **doesn't go well with, doesn't go with** : 잘 어울리지 않는다.

  clunky : 투박한
  Amish : 아미쉬파(현대 기술 문명을 거부하고 소박한 농경 생활을 하는 미국의 한 종교 집단)

⏱ Practice

1 너 셔츠랑 신발 잘 어울린다.

2 이 귀걸이 네 원피스랑 되게 잘 어울릴 것 같아.

3 햄버거는 감자튀김과 잘 어울려.

4 떡볶이랑 튀김은 잘 어울려요.

주요 장면 STUDY

Rachel   Marcel? Marcel. Marc.

Rachel   Marcel? 어디 갔어?

Joey   How could you lose him?

Joey   어떻게 잃어버려?

Rachel   I don't know. I don't know. We were watching TV, and then he <u>pooped</u> in Monica's shoe.

Rachel   나도 몰라. TV 보고 있었는데, Monica구두에 응가를 했더라고.

Monica   Wait. He pooped in my shoe? Which one?

Monica   잠깐, 내 신발에 응가를 했어? 어떤 거?

Rachel   I don't know. The left one.

Rachel   모르겠어. 왼쪽 같아.

Monica   Which ones?

Monica   어떤 신발이냐고.

Rachel   Oh. Oh, those little <u>clunky</u> <u>Amish</u> things you think go with everything.

Rachel   아, 아, 아무 옷에나 어울리는 줄 알고 신고 다니는 그 작고 투박한 신발 있잖아.

- poop : 응가를 하다
- clunky : 투박한
- Amish : 미국 동부에 근거한 매우 전통적인 기독교 종파.
- go with : 어울리다

run something by someone
(상대의) 생각을 물어보다

> **Ross** Uh, okay, yeah, we could do that, but before we <u>head off to</u> the murder capital of the North-East, I was, uh, kinda wanting to **run something by you**. You know how we were, uh, you know, talking before about, uh, relationships and stuff? Well.

> **Ross** 음, 좋아, 갈 수는 있지만, 북동부 위험 도시로 가기 전에, 너한테 묻고 싶은 말이 있었거든. 전에 했던 말인데, 남자 사귀는 문제 말이야.

📋 Note

• **run** : 달리다 / 상대의 의견을 묻다, 상의하다.

  (그냥 통보, 말하는 것이 아니라 의견을 묻고 상의하는 것)

• **run something by someone** : ~에 대하여 ~의 의견을 묻다

⏱ Practice

1 상사한테 먼저 의견을 물어보는 게 좋을 것 같아요.

2 부모님께 여쭤보는 게 어때?

3 그거 제출하기 전에 내 의견을 먼저 물어봐주세요.

4 내가 너한테 의견을 한번 구했어야 하는 건데.

👥주요 장면 STUDY

Ross Hey. How did, uh, how did it go today?

Ross 안녕. 오늘 어땠어?

Rachel Great! It went great. Really great. Hey, is that wine?

Rachel 좋았지! 정말 좋았어. 와, 이거 와인이야?

Ross Yeah. You, uh, you want some?

Ross 응, 마실래?

Rachel Oh, I would love some. But you know what? You know what? Let's not drink it here. I'm feeling kinda crazy. You wanna go to <u>Newark</u>?

Rachel 아, 마시고 싶지만, 근데 말이야, 있잖아, 여기서 마시지는 말자. 지금 기분이 좀 그래서. Newark 갈래?

Ross Uh, okay, yeah, we could do that, but before we <u>head off to</u> the murder capital of the North-East, I was, uh, kinda wanting to <u>run something by you</u>. You know how we were, uh, you know, talking before about, uh, relationships and stuff? Well.

Ross 음, 좋아, 갈 수는 있지만, 북동부 위험 도시로 가기 전에, 너한테 묻고 싶은 말이 있었거든. 전에 했던 말인데, 남자 사귀는 문제 말이야.

Rachel Oh God, Ross, I cannot do this.

Rachel 오 세상에, Ross, 나 안 되겠어.

Ross Okay, quick and painful.

Ross 그래, 대답 한번 빠르고 아프네.

• Newark : 미국 오하이오주 중부 도시. 인디언의 유적인 무덤이 많다
• head off to : ~로 향하다
• run something by someone : 누군가에게 생각을 묻다

say something to oneself
속으로 생각하다, 혼잣말하다

| Phoebe | Oh my God. You'd put that poor little <u>creature</u> in <u>jail</u>? |

| Phoebe | 세상에. 그 가엾은 동물을 감옥에 넣는다고요? |

| Monica | Pheebs, you remember how we talked about **saying things quietly to yourself first**? |

| Monica | Phoebe, 먼저 마음속으로 생각해보고 말하자고 했던 거 기억나? |

Note

• **say something to oneself** : 들리지 않게 혼잣말하다. 마음속으로 생각하다.

• **talk to oneself** : 혼자 말하다. 그냥 스스로에게 말하다.

Practice

1 그녀는 그냥 혼잣말한 것 같아.

2 너 뭐라고 혼잣말을 하는 거야?

3 그건 속으로 생각해야 할 것 같은데.

4 나는 스스로에게 계속할 수 있다고 말했어.

152

빵플릭스 1 **시즌 1** Episode 12~24

👥 주요 장면 STUDY

Monica Hi. We checked the third and fourth floor, no one's seen Marcel.

Monica 우리 3층하고 4층 체크해봤는데, Marcel 본 사람이 없어.

Luisa Marcel?

Luisa Marcel?

Ross My uncle Marcel.

Ross 아, 제 삼촌 Marcel이요.

Phoebe Oh, is that who the monkey's <u>named after</u>?

Phoebe 아, 원숭이 이름 지은 게 삼촌 이름을 딴 거였어?

Luisa Okay. <u>Are you aware</u> that <u>possession</u> of an <u>illegal</u> <u>exotic</u> is, uh, <u>punishable</u> by up to two years in prison and <u>confiscation</u> of the animal?

Luisa 좋아요. 불법 외래 동물 소유는 2년 이하 징역과 동물 압수로 처벌된다는 거 인지하고 있으신가요?

Phoebe Oh my God. You'd put that poor little <u>creature</u> in <u>jail</u>?

Phoebe 세상에. 그 가엾은 동물을 감옥에 넣는다고요?

Monica Pheebs, you remember how we talked about **saying things quietly to yourself first**?

Monica Phoebe, 먼저 마음속으로 생각해보고 말하자고 했던 거 기억나?

Phoebe Yes, but there isn't always time!

Phoebe 그래, 하지만 항상 그럴 시간이 있는 건 아니잖아.

- name after : 이름을 따다
- be aware : 인지하다
- possession : 소유
- illegal : 불법의
- exotic : 타국의, 이국적인

- punishable : 처벌할 수 있는
- confiscation : 몰수, 압류
- creature : 생물, 생명체
- * jail : 감옥

on purpose

일부러, 의도적으로

Rachel You know, it is not like I did this **on purpose**.

Rachel 있지, 내가 일부러 그런 것도 아니잖아.

Ross Oh, no, no, no. No no, this is just <u>vintage</u> Rachel.

Ross 아, 아냐, 아냐, 넌 원래 이런 식이야.

Note

• **purpose**

❶ 용도(What's the purpose of this object?)

❷ 목적(What's the purpose of taking this class?)

❸ 의도(What's the purpose of your action?)

• **do something on purpose** : 의도를 가지고 어떠한 행동을 하다.

↔ don't do it on purpose. : 의도를 가지고 하지 않다.

↔ do something on accident / by mistake : 사고나 실수로 고의나 의도 없이 어떠한 행동을 하다.

Practice

① 저 정말 의도적으로 한 게 아니에요.

② 지금 저를 의도적으로 피하시는 거예요?

③ 너 나랑 의도적으로 계속 마주치는 거지?

④ 내가 의도적으로 그렇게 문을 쾅 닫은 게 아니야.

주요 장면 STUDY

Ross Thank you very much.

Ross 아주 고맙다.

Rachel Ross, You know, I said I'm sorry like a million times. What do you want me to do? You want me to break my foot, too? Okay, I'm gonna break my foot, right here. Ow! Oh! Oh my God, oh my God! There, are you happy now?

Rachel Ross, 미안하다고 수백 번도 더 말했잖아. 내가 어떡했으면 좋겠어? 내 발도 다칠까? 그래, 내가 발이 다치면 되잖아. 아야, 아야, 아 진짜. 이제 만족해?

Ross Yeah, yeah. Y'know, now that you kicked the sign, hey! I don't miss Marcel any more!

Ross 응, 응, 너도 표지판 걷어차니까, Marcel이 더 이상 안 보고 싶다.

Rachel You know, it is not like I did this **on purpose**.

Rachel 있지, 내가 일부러 그런 것도 아니잖아.

Ross Oh, no, no, no. No no, this is just **vintage** Rachel.

Ross 아, 아냐, 아냐, 넌 원래 이런 식이야.

• on purpose : 의도적으로, 일부러
• vintage : 유서 깊은, 전통적인

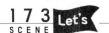
be hard on someone

~에게 심하게 대하다, 야박하게 굴다

> **Ross** Listen, I'm, I'm sorry **I was so hard on you** before, You know, I just.
>
> **Ross** 아까 너한테 심하게 군 거 미안해.
>
> **Rachel** Oh, Ross, come on. No, no, It's my fault, I <u>almost</u> lost your.
>
> **Rachel** 아, Ross, 괜찮아. 내 잘못인걸. 내가 잃어버릴 뻔했잖아.

Note

• **hard**

  1 어려운(hard to solve)

  2 단단하게, 엄하게(very strict)

  3 심하게, 가혹하게

• **be hard on someone** : 누군가에게 단단하게, 완고하게 구는 것

Practice

1 너무 심하게 혼내지 마. 아직 아기잖아.

2 우리 부모님은 우리를 엄하게 키우셨던 거 같아.

3 스스로에게 너무 엄하게 굴지 마.

4 네가 재능이 있어서 내가 더 엄하게 대했어.

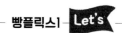

주요 장면 STUDY

Ross Listen, I'm, I'm sorry **I was so hard on you** before, You know, I just.

Ross 아까 너한테 심하게 군 거 미안해.

Rachel Oh, Ross, come on. No, no, It's my fault, I <u>almost</u> lost your.

Rachel 아, Ross, 괜찮아. 내 잘못인걸. 내가 잃어버릴 뻔했잖아.

Ross No, no, yeah, but you were the one who got him back, you know? You, you were great. Hey, we uh, we still have that, uh, that bottle of wine, You're in the mood for, uh, something grape?

Ross 아니야, 아니, 네가 다시 찾아 줬잖아. 정말 대단했어. 아, 우리 아직 와인 그대로 있는데, 한잔할까?

Rachel Sure, that'd be good.

Rachel 좋아, 마시자.

Ross Alright

Ross 좋아.

- be hard on someone : ~에게 심하게 대하다
- almost : 거의 ~하다, ~할 뻔하다
- be in the mood : ~할 생각이다, ~할 기분이다
- something grape : something great를 빗대서 와인을 의미함

needy

징징거리는, 애정을 갈구하는

> **Monica** So have you called her yet?
>
> **Monica** 그래서 전화했어?
>
> **Chandler** Let her know I like her? What are you, <u>insane</u>? It's the next day! How **needy** do I wanna seem? I'm right, right?
>
> **Chandler** 내가 좋아하는 거 알게? 미쳤어? 하루밖에 안 지났는데, 내가 얼마나 궁해 보이 겠어? 내가 맞는 거지? 맞지?

📓 Note

- **need** : 필요로 하다

- **needy**
  - **1** 무언가를 필요로 하는 / 애정에 굶주린 / 요구하는, 갈구하는
  - **2** 궁핍한, 가난한(needy children)

⏱ Practice

1 그만 좀 요구할래?

2 그가 너무 애정을 갈구해서 감당하기가 힘들어.

3 나는 애정을 갈구하는 쪽이 되고 싶지 않아.

4 한 번만 도와주면 이제 요구하지 않을게.

주요 장면 STUDY

Chandler It was unbelievable! We could totally be ourselves, we didn't have to play any games.

Chandler 믿기지가 않아. 우린 완전히 서로에게 솔직했어. 밀당 같은 거 할 필요도 없었어.

Monica So have you called her yet?

Monica 그래서 전화했어?

Chandler Let her know I like her? What are you, <u>insane</u>? It's the next day! How **needy** do I wanna seem? I'm right, right?

Chandler 내가 좋아하는 거 일게? 미쳤어? 하루밖에 안 시났는데, 내가 얼마나 궁해 보이겠어? 내가 맞는 거지? 맞지?

Joey and Ross Oh, yeah. Yeah. Let her dangle.

Joey and Ross 그래, 매달리게 해야지

- insane : 제정신이 아닌, 미친
- needy : 애정에 굶주린
- dangle : 매달리다

on the other line

통화 중이다

Chandler Danielle, hi! It's, uh, it's Chandler! I'm fine. Uh, listen, I don't know if you tried to call me, because, uh, idiot that I am, I <u>accidentally</u> shut off my phone. Oh, uh, okay, that's fine, that's great. Okay. <u>**She's on the other line**</u>, she's gonna call me back. She's on the other line, she's gonna call me back, she's on the other line, gonna call me back.

Chandler Danielle, 안녕! Chandler예요. 난 잘 지내요. 나한테 전화했는지 궁금해서 전화했어요. 왜냐하면, 바보처럼, 내 전화기를 우연히 꺼놨지 뭐예요. 아, 그래요, 그렇게 해요. 지금 통화 중이라고 다시 전화한대. 지금 통화 중이라고 다시 전화한대. 지금 통화 중이라고 다시 전화한대.

Note

• **line** : 영어에서 "전화상의 통화"라는 의미.

   e.g. Could you please stay on the line? = Could you please stay on the phone?

     : 끊지 말고 계셔주시겠어요?

     The line is busy. = 통화 중입니다.

     The person is on the other line =(다른 분과) 통화 중입니다.

⏱ Practice

1 내가 전화하려고 했는데 네가 통화 중이었어.

2 너는 왜 항상 통화 중이야?

3 전화 안 받는데, 아마 통화 중인 것 같아.

4 나 지금 통화 중이라 이따가 전화할게.

주요 장면 STUDY

Chandler Danielle, hi! It's, uh, it's Chandler! I'm fine. Uh, listen, I don't know if you tried to call me, because, uh, idiot that I am, I <u>accidentally</u> shut off my phone. Oh, uh, okay, that's fine, that's great. Okay. She's on the other line, she's gonna call me back. **She's on the other line**, she's gonna call me back, she's on the other line, gonna call me back.

Chandler Danielle, 안녕! Chandler예요. 난 잘 지내요. 나한테 전화했는지 궁금해서 전화했어요. 왜냐하면, 바보처럼, 내 전화기를 우연히 꺼놨지 뭐예요. 아, 그래요, 그렇게 해요. 지금 통화 중이라고 다시 전화한대. 지금 통화 중이라고 다시 전화한대. 지금 통화 중이라고 다시 전화한대

Monica Don't you have to pee?

Monica 화장실 가려던 거 아니었어?

Chandler That's why I'm dancing.

Chandler 그러니까 춤추고 있지.

• accidentally : 우연히
• on the other line : 통화 중인

see someone

~와 사귀다

> Rachel Oh, sure it is!
>
> Rachel 당연히 그게 다지, 왜!
>
> Mindy Oh no, it isn't! No! I think Barry is **seeing someone** in the city.
>
> Mindy 그게 다가 아냐. 내가 보기에 Barry가 여기서 바람피우는 거 같아.

 Note

• **see** : 계속해서 만남을 가지다(공식적인 관계는 아님)

• **see / dating > go out with a relationship with someone**

  (사귀는 것보다는 덜 진지한 형태)

• 보통 현재 진행 형태로 씀

  i.e I'm seeing someone / He is seeing someone.

Practice

1 나 요즘 만나는 사람이 있어.

2 누군가를 조금 만나보면 어때요?

3 그가 만나는 사람이 있는 것 같아?

4 나 너 말고 만나온 사람이 있어.

🐧🐧주요 장면 STUDY

| Mindy | Okay, I'm just gonna say it. |

| Mindy | 좋아, 그냥 말할게. |

| Rachel | Okay. |

| Rachel | 그래. |

| Mindy | Will you be my <u>maid of honour</u>? |

| Mindy | 내 들러리가 돼줄래? |

| Rachel | Of course! |

| Rachel | 물론이지! |

| Mindy | Oh that's so great! |

| Mindy | 아, 잘됐다! |

| Rachel | Was that all you wanted to ask me? |

| Rachel | 물어본다는 게 그것뿐이야? |

| Mindy | That's all! |

| Mindy | 그게 다야. |

| Rachel | Ohh! What? What? |

| Rachel | 아, 왜? 왜? |

| Mindy | That's not all. |

| Mindy | 그게 다가 아냐. |

| Rachel | Oh, sure it is! |

| Rachel | 당연히 그게 다지, 왜! |

| Mindy | Oh no, it isn't! No! I think Barry is **seeing someone** in the city. |

| Mindy | 그게 다가 아냐. 내가 보기에 Barry가 여기서 바람피우는 거 같아. |

• maid of honour : 결혼식장 들러리, 시녀
• see someone : ~를 만나다, 사귀다

can't help v-ing

~를 하지 않을 수 없다, 어쩔 수 없다

> **Mindy** <u>Basically</u>, we think you're a horrible human being, and bad things should happen to you.

> **Mindy** 우선, 자기는 나쁜 사람이야. 그리고 벌받아야 해.

> **Barry** I'm sorry, I'm sorry, God, I am so sorry, I'm an idiot, I was weak, **I couldn't help** myself! Whatever I did, I only did because I love you so much!

> **Barry** 미안해, 미안해. 세상에. 정말 미안해. 내가 바보였고, 너무 나약해. 어쩔 수가 없었다고. 무슨 짓을 했건, 당신을 너무 사랑했기 때문이야.

Note

- **can't help** = **be helpless** : 통제할 수 없다.
- **can't help myself.** : 스스로를 어쩔 수가 없다.
- **can't help 동-ing** : ~하지 않을 수 없다.
  ex can't help falling in love with you. = 사랑하지 않을 수 없다.

Practice

1 내 실수에 대한 생각을 안 할 수가 없어.

2 당신 생각을 도저히 안 할 수가 없어요.

3 그 남자 너무 잘 생겨서, 그를 쳐다볼 수밖에 없었어.

4 그들의 이야기를 안 들을 수가 없었어.

주요 장면 STUDY

Rachel Hey. Got a second?

Rachel 안녕, 시간 있어?

Barry Sure, sure. Come on in.

Barry 그럼, 그럼, 들어와.

Mindy Hello, sweetheart.

Mindy 안녕 자기.

Barry Uh uh what're you, what're you guys doing here?

Barry 아, 너희들 여기서 뭐 하려고?

Rachel Uh, we are here to break up with you.

Rachel 응, 우리 당신하고 헤어지려고.

Barry Both of you?

Barry 둘 다?

Mindy <u>Basically</u>, we think you're a horrible human being, and bad things should happen to you.

Mindy 우선, 자기는 나쁜 사람이야. 그리고 벌받아야 해.

Barry I'm sorry, I'm sorry, God, I am so sorry, I'm an idiot, I was weak, **I couldn't help** myself! Whatever I did, I only did because I love you so much!

Barry 미안해, 미안해. 세상에. 정말 미안해. 내가 바보였고, 너무 나약해. 어쩔 수가 없었다고. 무슨 짓을 했건, 당신을 너무 사랑했기 때문이야.

- basically : 기본적으로, 무엇보다도, 우선
- couldn't help ~ : ~하지 않을 수 없다, 어찌할 수 없다

run out on someone
~를 버리다

Monica	Really?
Monica	정말?
Rachel	Yeah! You know, ever since **I ran out on Barry** at the wedding, I have wondered whether I made the right choice. Uh, and now I know.
Rachel	응! 내가 결혼식장에서 Barry를 버린 후, 내가 잘한 선택인지 궁금했거든. 근데 이제 알겠어.

Note

- **run out** : 뛰쳐나가다

- **run out on someone** : 상대를 둔 채로 뛰쳐나가다

  » 단순히 '두고 가다'라는 의미 이외에 책임져야 할 상대를 완전히 버리다

  (abandon someone, desert someone)는 뜻

Practice

1 네가 나를 버리고 가다니 믿을 수가 없어.

2 네가 나를 버린 것을 용서하지 않을 거야.

3 내 남자친구가 바람피운다는 사실을 알았을 때 그를 버렸어.

4 그의 부모님은 그가 어렸을 때 그를 버리고 떠나셨어.

👥 주요 장면 STUDY

| Monica | You okay? |

| Monica | 괜찮아? |

| Rachel | Yeah. |

| Rachel | 그럼. |

| Monica | Really? |

| Monica | 정말? |

| Rachel | Yeah! You know, ever since **I ran out on Barry** at the wedding, I have wondered whether I made the right choice. Uh, and now I know. |

| Rachel | 응! 내가 결혼식장에서 Barry를 버린 후, 내가 잘한 선택인지 궁금했거든. 근데 이제 알겠어. |

| Monica | Aww. |

| Monica | 아. |

| Joey | Big day. |

| Joey | 대박이네. |

• run out on someone : ~를 버리다, ~를 두고 도망 나오다

lose it

(화, 웃음 등을) 참지 못하다, 이성을 잃다

> **Monica** This woman got my life, I should get to see who she is.
>
> **Monica** 이 여자는 내 인생을 살고 있어. 직접 가서 누군지 보고 싶어.
>
> **Rachel** Okay, Monica, you know what, honey, **you're kinda losing it here**! I mean, this is really becoming like a weird <u>obsession</u> thing.
>
> **Rachel** 좋아, Monica, 있잖아, 넌 지금 약간 제정신이 아닌 것 같아. 그러니까, 그러다 진짜 편집증으로 흐를 수 있어.

📋 Note

- lose = ~를 잃다 / it이 가르키는 건 '정신' one's mind
- lose it = lose one's mind : 화나 웃음 등 어떤 감정을 참지 못할 때 / 너무 화가 나거나 너무 웃거나 제정신이 아닌 행동을 할 때

  i.e You're losing it / I'm losing it. = 너 / 나 약간 정신 나갔어.

🕐 Practice

1 진정해. 너 제정신이 아닌 것 같아.

2 그녀가 내 탓을 했을 때 나는 완전 이성을 잃었어.

3 질문 한 개만 더 하면 나 이성을 잃을 것 같아.

4 내 감정을 참으려고 했는데 결국 터져버렸어.

주요 장면 STUDY

Monica Alright, great. great. Thanks a lot. I'm going to tap class.

Monica 네, 좋아요, 네, 감사합니다. 나 탭댄스 배울 거야.

Rachel What, what, so that you can dance with the woman that <u>stole</u> your credit card?

Rachel 뭐, 뭐, 네 신용카드 훔친 여자랑 춤을 추겠다는 거야?

Monica I wanna see what she looks like.

Monica 어떻게 생겼는지 보고 싶어.

Rachel Well then just go to the post office! I'm sure they got her picture up!

Rachel 그러면 우체국을 가. 거기에 그 여자 사진 붙어 있을 거야.

Monica This woman got my life, I should get to see who she is.

Monica 이 여자는 내 인생을 살고 있어. 직접 가서 누군지 보고 싶어.

Rachel Okay, Monica, you know what, honey, **you're kinda losing it here**! I mean, this is really becoming like a weird <u>obsession</u> thing.

Rachel 좋아, Monica, 있잖아, 넌 지금 약간 제정신이 아닌 것 같아. 그러니까, 그러다 진짜 편집증으로 흐를 수 있어.

Phoebe This is madness. It's madness, I tell you, <u>for the love of God</u>, Monica, don't do it!

Phoebe 이건 광기야. 광기. 제발, Monica, 이러지 마!

- tap : 톡톡 두드리다, 박자를 맞추다
- steal : 훔치다 steal – stole – stolen
- lose it : 이성을 잃다, 정신이 나가다
- obsession : 강박 관념, 집착
- for the love of God : 제발

169

get something

이해하다

> **Monica** Okay, **I'm not getting this!**
>
> **Monica** 근데, 나는 뭐가 뭔지 모르겠어!
>
> **Phoebe** I'm totally getting it!
>
> **Phoebe** 난 너무 잘하는 거 같은데!

Note

- **get**

  » get은 표준, formal 단어이지만 'understand'라는 의미의 get은 slang / 비격식적 표현

  1 가지다, 얻다(I got this for you.)

  2 이해하다, 파악하다.(I got it. / Did you get it?)

- **Gotcha = Get you!** = 너를 이해했어 = 네가 하는 말을 이해했어(알겠어)

Practice

1 너 이 문제 이해돼?

2 나 이해 못 한 것 같아.

3 내가 왜 화났는지 이해가 돼?

4 네가 하는 말 다 이해했어.

🗣️주요 장면 STUDY

Teacher Let's get started. Five, six, five, six, seven, eight.

Teacher 시작합시다. 5, 6, 5, 6, 7,8

Monica Okay, I'm not getting this!

Monica 근데, 나는 뭐가 뭔지 모르겠어!

Phoebe **I'm totally getting it!**

Phoebe 난 너무 잘하는 거 같은데!

Monica Did you ever feel like sometimes you are just so unbelievably uncoordinated?

Monica 너희들 가끔 몸이 제각각 움직이는 것 같은 기분 든 적 없니?

Rachel What? You just click when they click.

Rachel 뭐? 남들 할 때 똑같이 따라 하면 돼.

- get something: 이해하다
- uncoordinated : 균형 잡히지 못한, 조직적이 아닌
- click : 딸깍 소리를 내다

make fool of oneself

바보짓을 하다, 웃음거리가 되다

Monica Excuse me?

Monica 뭐라고?

Fake Monica There's <u>an open call</u> for Cats. I'm thinking we go down there, sing Memories and **make complete fools of ourselves**. <u>What did you say?</u>

Fake Monica 'Cats' 공개 오디션이 있어. 우리 거기 가서, 'Memories' 노래를 부르고, 완전히 웃음거리가 되는 거야. 어때?

Note

- **fool** = 멍청한 사람, 어리석은 사람
- **foolish** = 어리석은, 멍청한
- **make a fool of oneself** = 본인을 웃음거리로 만들다(스스로)
- **make a fool(out) of someone** = ~를 망신주다

Practice

1 나 지금 완전 바보짓 하는 것 같아.

2 나는 웃음거리가 되고 싶지 않으니까 노래하지 않을 거야.

3 너 지금 술 취해서 바보짓 하고 있어.

4 그가 내 친구들 앞에서 나를 완전 망신 줬어.

주요 장면 STUDY

Fake Monica Oh, by the way, tomorrow we're auditioning for a Broadway show.

Fake Monica 아, 근데, 내일 우리 브로드웨이 쇼 오디션 보러 갈 거야.

Monica Excuse me?

Monica 뭐라고?

Fake Monica There's <u>an open call</u> for Cats. I'm thinking we go down there, sing Memories and **make complete fools of ourselves**. <u>What do you say?</u>

Fake Monica 'Cats' 공개 오디션이 있어. 우리 거기 가서, 'Memories' 노래를 부르고, 완전히 웃음거리가 되는 거야. 어때?

Monica No, no, no, no. Remember who you're <u>dealing with</u> here. I mean, I'm not like you. I can't even stand in front of a tap class.

Monica 아니, 아니, 네가 말하고 있는 사람이 누군지 모르나 본데, 그러니까, 난 네가 아냐. 난 탭댄스 수업에서 앞 줄에 서지도 못하잖아.

- audition : 오디션을 보다
- an open call : 공개 모집 오디션
- make a fool of : 웃음거리가 되다, 바보짓을 하다
- What did you say? : 어때?
- deal with : 다루다, 대하다

show up
나타나다

Rachel	Yes, yes, it does. Okay, look, the restaurant called again today, they wanna know if you're gonna be **showing up** for work?
Rachel	그래, 그래, 좋지. 오늘 또 식당에서 전화 왔어. 네가 출근할 건지 알고 싶대.
Monica	Nope. Going to the Big Apple Circus today.
Monica	아니, 안 가. 오늘 뉴욕 서커스에 가기로 했거든.

 Note

[구분!]

• **show up** : 보여주다, 드러내다

　ie I'm showing up today. : 오늘 갈 거야.

• **show off** : 자랑하다.

　ie I wanna show off my new jacket. : 내 자켓 자랑하고 싶어.

Practice

☐ 그녀는 이번 주 내내 회사에 나오지 않았어.

☐ 오늘도 안 오면 너 잘릴 거야.

☐ 그녀는 영화가 끝날 때까지 나타나지 않았어.

☐ 네가 갑자기 TV에서 나와서 놀랐어.

주요 장면 STUDY

Rachel | Monica? Monica!

Rachel | Monica? Monica!

Monica | Water rules!

Monica | 물 짱 좋아!

Rachel | Yes, yes, it does. Okay, look, the restaurant called again today, they wanna know if you're gonna be <u>**showing up**</u> for work?

Rachel | 그래, 그래, 좋지. 오늘 또 식당에서 전화 왔어. 네가 출근할 건지 알고 싶대.

Monica | Nope. Going to <u>the Big Apple Circus</u> today.

Monica | 아니, 안 가. 오늘 뉴욕 서커스에 가기로 했거든.

Rachel | Okay Monica, what are you doing? You're gonna lose your job! This is not you!

Rachel | 자, Monica, 너 지금 뭐 하는 거야? 그러다가 너 실직할 거야. 이건 네 모습이 아니라고!

Monica | No, it is me!

Monica | 아니, 이게 나야!

• water rules : 물 짱 좋아, 물 맛 죽여준다
• show up : 나타나다, 출현하다
• the Big Apple Circus : 뉴욕에서 하는 서커스

turn someone in

~를 고발하다, 신고하다

> Monica I want you to know, it wasn't me **who turned you in**.
>
> Monica 내가 신고한 게 아니란 것만 알아줘.
>
> Fake Monica Oh. Thanks.
>
> Fake Monica 고마워.

Note

- **turn in** : 내다, 제출하다, 반납하다

  i.e turn in your homework / turn in your test papers

- **turn someone in** : 어떤 사람을 내주다(**hand someone over to the police**)

  고발하다, 신고하다

- **turn oneself in** = 자수하다

Practice

1 나 너를 신고할 거야.

2 난 정말 너를 신고하고 싶지 않지만, 그래야만 해.

3 경찰이 너를 잡기 전에 자수하는 게 좋을 것 같아.

4 나는 절대 자수하지 않을 거야.

👥 주요 장면 STUDY

Monica Hi.

Monica 안녕.

Fake Monica Hey.

Fake Monica 안녕.

Monica How are you?

Monica 좀 어때?

Fake Monica I'm not too bad. Fortunately, blue's my colour. How, how did you know I was here?

Fake Monica 그렇게 나쁘지는 않아. 다행히 파란색 좋아하거든. 나 여기 있는 건 어떻게 알았어?

Monica Because I'm Monica Geller. It was my credit card you were using.

Monica 실은 내가 Monica Geller야. 네가 쓰고 다닌 게 내 카드였고.

Fake Monica That I was not <u>expecting</u>.

Fake Monica 예상도 못했네.

Monica I want you to know, it wasn't me **who turned you in**.

Monica 내가 신고한 게 아니란 것만 알아줘.

Fake Monica Oh. Thanks.

Fake Monica 고마워.

Monica No, thank you! You have given me so much!

Monica 아니, 내가 고맙지! 내가 많은 걸 얻었어!

• expect : 예상하다, 기대하다

• turn someone in : ~를 고발하다, 신고하다

take a moment

~할 시간을 갖다

> **Ross** Uh, if you guys don't mind, **I'd like to take a moment**, just me and him.
>
> **Ross** 아, 괜찮으면, 단둘이 있게 해줄래?
>
> **All** Oh, sure. Sure, absolutely.
>
> **All** 아, 그럼, 그럼, 물론이지.

📝 Note

- **moment**

  ❶ 어떤 순간(happy moment / sad moment)

  ❷ 잠깐, 잠시(do something for a moment)

- **have / take a moment to ~** : 짬을 내어 ~하다, ~할 시간을 가지다

- '**I'd like to**' 는 '**I want to**' 보다 더 예의 바른 표현.

⏱ Practice

❶ 잠깐 진정할 시간을 좀 갖는 게 좋을 거 같아.

❷ 우리 관계에 대해 생각할 시간이 필요한 거 같아.

❸ 잠시 지난 미팅 내용을 복기하는 시간을 갖고 싶은데요.

❹ 잠시 저를 소개하는 시간을 갖고 싶어요.

🗣 주요 장면 STUDY

| Joey | I don't what to say, Ross. Uh, it's a monkey. |

| Joey | 뭐라고 해야 할지 모르겠어, Ross. 원숭이잖아! |

| Ross | Just, just say what you feel, Joey. |

| Ross | 그냥, 그냥 느끼는 대로 말해, Joey. |

| Joey | Marcel, I'm hungry. |

| Joey | Marcel, 나 배고파. |

| Ross | That was good |

| Ross | 좋아. |

| Rachel | Marcel, this is for you. It's, uh, just, you know, something to, um, do on the plane. |

| Rachel | Marcel, 이건 네 거야. 비행기에서 심심할까봐. |

| Ross | Uh, if you guys don't mind, **I'd like to take a moment**, just me and him. |

| Ross | 아, 괜찮으면, 잠시만 단둘이 있게 해줄래? |

| All | Oh, sure. Sure, absolutely. |

| All | 아, 그럼, 그럼, 물론이지. |

• take a moment : ~할 시간을 갖다

pass for

~로 통하다

| Monica | Oh, **I can't pass for 22**? |

| Monica | 나 22살처럼 안 보인다고? |

| Phoebe | Well, maybe 25-26. |

| Phoebe | 글쎄, 뭐 25살이나 26살 정도? |

Note

- **pass** : 통과하다, 합격하다, 지나가다.
- **pass for ~** : ~로서(진실인 양) 통하다, 인정받다, 넘어가다.

Practice

1 그녀는 너무 어려 보여서 10대라고 해도 믿을 것 같아.

2 나 20살처럼 보일 것 같아?

3 너 영어 정말 잘한다! 원어민이라고 해도 믿을 것 같아.

4 그녀는 이 분야에 대해서 아무것도 모르지만 전문가라고 불려.

주요 장면 STUDY

Monica Yeah, well, he's smart, and <u>mature</u> and <u>grown-up</u>.

Monica 그래, 걔는 똑똑하고, 성숙한 어른이야.

Ross Mature and grown up, He's a big boy.

Ross 성숙한 어른? 정말 다 컸네.

Chandler And this man child <u>has no problem with</u> how old you are?

Chandler 근데 그 아이는 네가 몇 살이든 상관없대?

Monica No, of course not. It's not even an issue. Cause I told him I was 22.

Monica 응, 당연하지. 그건 문제도 안 돼. 내가 22살이라고 했거든.

All What?

All 뭐라고?

Monica Oh, **I can't pass for 22**?

Monica 나 22살처럼 안 보인다고?

Phoebe Well, maybe 25-26.

Phoebe 글쎄, 뭐 25살이나 26살 정도?

Monica I am 26.

Monica 나 26살이잖아.

Phoebe There you go.

Phoebe 맞혔네!

- mature : 성숙한
- grown-up : 성인
- have no problem with ~ : ~와 상관없다, 문제가 안 된다

- an issue : 문제, 이야깃거리
- pass for : ~로 통하다

181

in / with reference to

~와 관련하여

> Chandler I'm not in a meeting. I'm right. Whoops.
>
> Chandler 나 회의 없잖아, 여기 있는데.
>
> Phoebe Will he know **what this is in reference to**? And he has your number? All right, I'll see that he <u>gets the message</u>. Bye bye.
>
> Phoebe 이것과 관련해서 Bing 씨가 아실까요? 그쪽 번호도 아시죠? 좋아요. 메시지 전해드릴게요. 감사합니다.

📋 Note

- **in reference to** : ~와 관련된(= **about**)

  🔢 Will he know what this is in reference to? = Will he know what this is about?

- **in reference to**를 주로 쓰는 경우

  1 상황에 따라 조금 더 격식을 갖춰야 하거나
  2 비즈니스 같은 일상에서 조금 다르게 말하고 싶을 때.
  3 말의 품격을 높여주는 표현들 중 하나.
  >> with reference to라고 쓰기도 함.

⏱ Practice

1 무엇에 관한 전화인지 알 수 있을까요?

2 당신의 제안에 대해 이메일을 드립니다.

3 오늘 미팅과 관련해서 드릴 말씀이 있는데요.

4 그것에 관해서는 드릴 말씀이 없네요.

주요 장면 STUDY

Phoebe Oh. Uh, I'm on.

Phoebe 아, 아, 내가 받을게.

Phoebe Mr. Bing's office. No, I'm sorry, he's in a meeting right now.

Phoebe Bing 사무실입니다. 아니에요. 죄송하지만, 지금 회의 참석 중이세요.

Chandler I'm not in a meeting. I'm right. Whoops.

Chandler 나 회의 없잖아, 여기 있는데.

Phoebe Will he know **what this is in reference to**? And he has your number? All right, I'll see that he <u>gets the message</u>. Bye bye.

Phoebe 이것과 관련해서 Bing 씨가 아실까요? 그쪽 번호도 아시죠? 좋아요. 메시지 전해 드릴게요. 감사합니다.

- in reference to ~ : ~와 관련해서
- get the message : 메시지를 받다

a touch

약간, 조금

> **Rachel** **Just a touch.** Mon, I don't understand. I mean, you've been dating this guy since like, what his <u>midterms</u>? I mean, why all the sudden are you so. Oh.
>
> **Rachel** 약간. 난 이해가 안 가. 이 친구랑 데이트한 게, 중간고사부터야? 그런데 왜 갑자기 그렇게. 아.
>
> **Monica** What?
>
> **Monica** 뭐?

Note

- **touch** : 🔵 만지다. 🔴 조금, 약간(**a small amount**)

- **just a touch** : 아주 조금 = **just a little** = **just a tad**

  » just 같이 쓰이면 조금 더 자연스럽고 '아주' 조금, 약간이라고 해석됨

⏱ Practice

🟦 너 지금 약간 정신없는 것 같아.

🟦 내 커피에 설탕 조금만 넣어줘.

🟦 네 것이 아주 조금 더 단 거 같아.

🟦 너는 단지 아주 조금 더 나보다 클 뿐이야.

주요 장면 STUDY

Monica Ok. Windows are clean, candles are lit. Uh, belt's too tight, gotta change the belt. Did I turn the fish? No, cause I made <u>Lasagne</u>. Am I <u>out of control</u>?

Monica 좋아, 창문은 깨끗하고, 촛불도 켰고, 벨트가 너무 조여. 바꿔야겠다. 생선은 뒤집었나? 참, 라자냐 만들고 있었지. 내가 너무 정신없나?

Rachel **Just a touch**. Mon, I don't understand. I mean, you've been dating this guy since like, what his <u>midterms</u>? I mean, why all the sudden are you so. Oh.

Rachel 약간. 넌 이해가 안 가. 이 친구랑 데이느힌 게, 중간고시 뿌니야? 그런데에 갑시기 그렇게. 아.

Monica What?

Monica 뭐?

Rachel Could tonight be the Night?

Rachel 오늘 밤이 그 밤인가?

- lit : light의 과거형(light-lit-lit)
- light : 불을 붙이다
- Lasagne : 라자냐. 이탈리아 요리.
- out of control : 정신없는, 통제 불능의
- a touch : 약간, 조금
- midterm : 중간고사

used to

예전에는 ~했다, ~하곤 했다

Chandler What are you talking about?

Chandler 무슨 말 하는 거야?

Phoebe Don't feel bad. You know **they used to like you** a lot. But then you got promoted, and, you know, now you're like "Mr. Boss Man". You know, Mr. Bing. Mr. Bing, "Boss Man Bing".

Phoebe 기분 상하지 마. 예전에는 너를 많이 좋아했었대. 하지만, 네가 승진한 후로는, 지금은 네가 너무 "상사" 같다는 거야. Bing 상사 노릇!

 Note

- 'used to' 주의할 사항 3가지

  1 발음할 때 "t"와 "d"가 한꺼번에 발음됨 - 들리기에는 'use to' 처럼 들림.

  2 과거에는 그랬는데 현재는 그렇지 않다는 뜻.

  ≫ I used to like you.(과거에는 너를 좋아했었지. 지금은 아니지만.)

  ≫ I used to be good at something.(과거에는 ~를 잘 했었지. 지금은 아니지만.)

  3 used to(~하곤 했다) vs. be used to(~에 적응하다)

⏱ Practice

1 나 예전에는 영어 잘했는데 이젠 아니야.

2 나 예전에는 커피를 열 잔씩 마셨어.

3 우리 예전에 가까운 사이였어.

4 우리 예전에는 훨씬 더 자주 봤었는데.

주요 장면 STUDY

Phoebe They don't like you.

Phoebe 직원들이 널 싫어해.

Chandler What?

Chandler 뭐?

Phoebe I thought you knew that.

Phoebe 네가 아는 줄 알았는데.

Chandler Noho. Who doesn't like me?

Chandler 아아니. 누가 나를 싫어하는데?

Phoebe Everyone. Except for, uh no! everyone.

Phoebe 모두 다. 누군 아니었는데, 아니다. 모두 다야.

Chandler What are you talking about?

Chandler 무슨 말 하는 거야?

Phoebe Don't feel bad. You know **they used to like you** a lot. But then you got promoted, and, you know, now you're like "Mr. Boss Man". You know, Mr. Bing. Mr. Bing, "Boss Man Bing".

Phoebe 기분 상하지 마. 예전에는 너를 많이 좋아했었대. 하지만, 네가 승진한 후로는, 지금은 네가 너무 "상사" 같다는 거야. Bing 상사 노릇!

• except for ~ : ~는 제외하고
• used to : 예전에는 ~했다, ~하곤 했다

187

be in charge(of) ~

~에 대해 책임, 권한이 있다

> **Phoebe** No, I know. That's a part of the whole, you know, them-not-liking-you-<u>extravaganza</u>.

> **Phoebe** 응, 알아. 일종의 '너를 싫어하는 사람들'의 모임이니까.

> **Chandler** You know, I don't get this. A month ago, these people were my friends. You know, just because **I'm in charge** doesn't mean I'm a different person.

> **Chandler** 이해가 안 돼. 한 달 전만 해도, 여기 동료들은 내 친구였다고. 내가 승진했다고 딴 사람이 된 건 아니잖아.

Note

- **the person in charge** = 책임자

- **be in charge of something** = ~를 담당하다.

- **put someone in charge of something.** = ~에게 ~의 책임을 맡기다

Practice

1 제가 이 사무실의 책임자입니다.

2 이 프로젝트 총책임자가 누구죠?

3 그녀가 나한테 된장찌개를 맡겼어.

4 나는 아무것도 담당하고 싶지 않아.

👥 주요 장면 STUDY

Rachel Where are you going?

Rachel 어디 가는데?

Phoebe Um, oh, I've got a birthday party with some work people.

Phoebe 아, 생일 파티가 있어. 회사 동료들하고.

Chandler Work people? Nobody told me.

Chandler 회사 동료들? 아무도 나한테는 말 안 하던데.

Phoebe No, I know. That's a part of the whole, you know, them-not-liking-you-<u>extravaganza</u>.

Phoebe 응, 알아. 일종의 '너를 싫어하는 사람들'의 모임이니까.

Chandler You know, I don't get this. A month ago, these people were my friends. You know, just because **I'm in charge** doesn't mean I'm a different person.

Chandler 이해가 안 돼. 한 달 전만 해도, 여기 동료들은 내 친구였다고. 내가 책임자가 되었다고 딴 사람이 된 건 아니잖아.

- extravaganza : 화려한 오락거리.
- be in charge : ~에 대해 책임이 있다, 권한이 있다

icky

끈적한, 찝찝한

Young Ethan Then, what's the problem?

Young Ethan 그러면 뭐가 문제예요?

Monica Ethan, it's um, **it's icky.**

Monica Ethan, 그게 좀 찝찝해.

 Note

• **icky**

  1 끈적거리다.(촉감)

  2 불쾌하다, 찝찝하다, 징그럽다.(상황)

  3 역겹다.(맛)

Practice

1 그거 만지지 마! 좀 끈적거려.

2 내 신발에 끈적한 뭐가 묻은 것 같아.

3 이 음식 역겨워. 먹을 수가 없어.

4 나보다 훨씬 나이가 어린 사람이랑 사귀는 건 징그러워.

주요 장면 STUDY

Young Ethan Then, what's the problem?

Young Ethan 그러면 뭐가 문제예요?

Monica Ethan, it's um, **it's icky**.

Monica Ethan, 그게, 좀 찝찝해.

Young Ethan Icky? You're actually gonna throw this away because it's icky?

Young Ethan 찝찝하다고? 찝찝하다는 이유로 우리 관계를 끝낸다고요?

Monica This isn't easy for me, either. I wish things were different, I, If you were a few years older, or if I was a few years younger, or if we lived in <u>biblical times</u>, I would really.

Monica 나에게도 쉬운 일은 아니야. 나도 상황이 좀 달랐으면 해. 네가 몇 살 위든가, 내가 몇 살 아래든가, 아니면 우리가 몇 천 년 전에 살았든가. 난 정말.

Young Ethan No, don't say it.

Young Ethan 아니, 말하지 말아요.

Monica love you.

Monica 사랑했을 거야.

• icky : 끈적한, 찝찝한
• biblical times : 성서 시대의

191

phone person

통화를 좋아하는 사람

> **Joey** Hi, yeah, it's me. Oh, no, no, no, we're just friends. Yeah, I'm single. 25. An actor. Hello?
>
> **Joey** 안녕하세요. 저예요. 오, 아니요, 아니요, 저희 그냥 친구예요. 네, 저는 결혼 안 했고요. 25살이고 배우입니다. 여보세요?
>
> **Lydia** She's not much of **a phone person**.
>
> **Lydia** 엄마가 그렇게 통화를 별로 안 좋아해서요.

Note

- **not much of ~** : ~를 별로 아니다.

- **~ person** : ~를 좋아하는 사람, ~한 사람

- **phone person** = 통화를 좋아하는 사람 / **text person** = 문자를 좋아하는 사람

Practice

1 그녀는 진짜 통화를 좋아하는 사람이 아니야. 전화 절대 안 받아.

2 너 통화 안 좋아하는 거 알지만 그래도 가끔 전화 줘.

3 저는 통화보다는 문자를 좋아하는 사람이에요.

4 저는 통화를 별로 안 좋아하는데, 문자로 해도 괜찮을까요?

🗣 주요 장면 STUDY

| Lydia | Mom, we've been through this. No, I'm not calling him. I don't care if it is his kid, the guy's a <u>jerk</u>. No, I'm not alone. Joey's here. What do you mean, Joey who? Joey who?

| Lydia | 엄마, 우리는 완전히 끝났어요. 싫어요, 전화 안 해요. 그 사람 아이여도 상관 안 해요. 그 사람은 그냥 얼간이예요. 아니에요, 혼자 아니에요. Joey가 있어요. Joey가 누구냐고요?

| Joey | Tribbiani.

| Joey | Tribbiani.

| Lydia | Joey Tribbiani. Yes, ok. Hold on. She wants to talk to you. Take the phone.

| Lydia | Joey Tribbiani예요. 네. 잠깐만요. 전화 바꿔 달래요. 전화 받아요.

| Joey | Hi, yeah, it's me. Oh, no, no, no, we're just friends. Yeah, I'm single. 25. An actor. Hello?

| Joey | 안녕하세요. 저예요. 오, 아니요, 아니요, 저희 그냥 친구예요. 네, 저는 결혼 안 했고요. 25살이고 배우입니다. 여보세요?

| Lydia | She's not much of **a phone person**.

| Lydia | 엄마가 그렇게 통화를 별로 안 좋아해서요.

| Joey | Yeah.

| Joey | 네.

• jerk : 얼간이, 멍청이
• phone person : 통화를 좋아하는 사람, 통화를 잘하는 사람.

check up on someone / something

~를 살피다, 확인하다

Dr. Franzblau **I'm gonna go check up on your friend.**

Dr. Franzblau 친구분 상태 좀 보러 가야겠네요.

Rachel Ok. That's fine.

Rachel 네, 그러세요.

 Note

["check" vs. "check up on"]

» check : 단순히 무언가를 확인. '무엇'을 확인하는지 명시해야 함(**i.e** Check if he is doing okay.)

» check up on someone / something : 사람이나 일이 잘되고 있는지, 상태가 괜찮은지 확인하다.

cf get a check-up, get checked up : 건강검진 받다.

Practice

1 신입사원 잘 하고 있는지 자주 확인 좀 해줘.

2 그냥 네가 잘하고 있는지 확인하려고 왔어.

3 먼저 몇 가지 좀 확인 해야 할 사항이 있어요.

4 그 프로젝트가 잘 진행되고 있는지 확인하려고 전화했어요.

👥 주요 장면 STUDY

Dr. Franzblau Well, for instance, what do you do?

Dr. Franzblau 근데, 무슨 일 하세요?

Rachel I'm a waitress.

Rachel 아, 저는 웨이트리스예요.

Dr. Franzblau Ok, all right, well aren't there times when you come home at the end of the day, and you're just like, 'if I see one more cup of coffee…'

Dr. Franzblau 네, 좋아요, 퇴근 후 집에 가면 '내가 만약 커피 한 잔 더 보기라도 한다면' 이럴 때 없나요?

Rachel Yeah. Gotcha.

Rachel 아, 알겠네요.

Dr. Franzblau **I'm gonna go check up on your friend.**

Dr. Franzblau 친구분 상태 좀 보러 가야겠네요.

Rachel Ok. That's fine.

Rachel 네, 그러세요.

• gotcha : 알겠다, 이해했다, 'I've got you' 의 줄임말
• check up on someone : ~상태를 살피다

cook something up

꾸며내다, 지어내다

> **Carol** Ben. Ben. Ben's good. How come you never mentioned Ben before?
>
> **Carol** Ben. Ben. Ben이 좋겠어. 어째서 Ben은 말하지 않았지?
>
> **Ross** We uh, **we just cooked it up**.
>
> **Ross** 우리가 그냥 방금 지어낸 거야.

Note

• **cook** : 요리하다

• **cook up something** : 요리를 재빠르게 하다. 무언가를 빨리 지어내다

 (보통은 남을 속이기 위해 무언가를 빨리 지어낼 때, 계획을 꾸밀 때)

Practice

1 우리 어떤 변명거리라도 지금 만들어보자.

2 우리 지금 완전 믿을 만한 변명거리를 만들어낸 것 같아.

3 너 그거 방금 만들어낸 얘기지?

4 사실 그거 그냥 만들어낸 이야기야.

👥 주요 장면 STUDY

Susan	We still need a name for this little guy.
Susan	아기 이름 지어야 해.
Ross	How about Ben?
Ross	Ben 어때요?
Susan	I like Ben.
Susan	Ben 좋은데요.
Carol	Ben. Ben. Ben's good. How come you never mentioned Ben before?
Carol	Ben. Ben. Ben이 좋겠어. 어째서 Ben은 말하지 않았지?
Ross	We uh, **we just cooked it up**.
Ross	우리가 그냥 방금 지어낸 거야.
Susan	That's what we were off doing.
Susan	그러느라 나가 있었어.
Monica	Hi.
Monica	저기.
Ross	Hey.
Ross	안녕.
Monica	Can we come in?
Monica	들어가도 돼?
Ross	Come in.
Ross	들어 와.
Ross	I know, I know. Everybody, there's someone I'd like you to meet. Yeah. This is Ben. Ben, this is everybody.
Ross	그래, 그래. 여러분 소개할 사람이 있어요. 여기는 Ben이예요. Ben, 친구들이야.
Phoebe	Susan, he looks just like you.
Phoebe	Susan, 당신을 꼭 닮았네요.
Susan	Thanks.
Susan	고마워요.

• cook something up : 방금 꾸며내다, 지어내다

look out for someone

~를 지키다, 보살피다, 조심하다

> Ross Yeah. I guess. I don't, I don't know. Alright, just, just give her this for me, OK?
>
> Ross 그래야겠지. 모르겠어. 이거나 대신 전해줘. 알았지?
>
> Joey Listen, buddy, **we're just looking out for you.**
>
> Joey 친구. 우리가 지킬게.

 Note

- **look out for something**
  - ❶ 무엇인가를 피하기 위해서 조심하다. (Look out for bugs here.)
  - ❷ 무엇인가를 찾기 위해서 주의하다. (Look out for a green bicycle.)

- **look out for someone**
  - » 누군가를 지키기 위해서 보살피다, 주시하다.

Practice

❶ 어른이니까 스스로를 보살펴야 돼요.

❷ 네가 오빠니까 동생을 돌봐줘야 해.

❸ 유럽에서는 소매치기를 조심해야 해.

❹ 저랑 같이 빨간 차를 주의해서 찾아주실 수 있을까요?

🗣️ 주요 장면 STUDY

Ross Well, Rachel's having drinks with him tonight.

Ross 그게, Rachel이 오늘 밤 그 남자하고 술 마신대.

Joey Oh no! How can she do that when she's never shown any interest in you?

Joey 말도 안 돼! 너한테는 관심도 없으면서 어떻게 그럴 수 있지?

Chandler Forget about her.

Chandler 잊어버려.

Joey He's right, man. Please. <u>Move on</u>. Go to China. Eat Chinese food.

Joey 맞아. 제발. 미련 좀 버려. 중국으로 그냥 가. 중국 음식도 좀 먹고.

Chandler Course there, they just call it food.

Chandler 물론 거기에선, '중국 음식'이 아니라 그냥 음식이라고 하겠지.

Ross Yeah. I guess. I don't, I don't know. Alright, just, just give her this for me, OK?

Ross 그래야겠지. 모르겠어. 이거나 대신 전해줘. 알았지?

Joey Listen, buddy, **we're just looking out for you**.

Joey 친구. 우리는 그냥 너 걱정하는거야.

Ross I know.

Ross 알아.

Joey We want you to be happy.

Joey 네가 행복하길 바라.

• move on : 이동하다, 전 연인에 대한 미련을 버리다
• look out for someone : ~를 지키다, 보살피다

hold up

버티다, 견디다

Monica Hey, hold on there, tiger. How's it going? **How you holding up?**

Monica 잠깐 이리 와봐. 어때? 잘 돼가고 있어?

Joey Well, not so good. She <u>definitely</u> thinks tonight is the night we're gonna <u>complete</u> the <u>transaction</u>, if you know what I.

Joey 글쎄, 감이 안 좋아. 그녀가 오늘 밤 우리 관계를 완성할 거라고 분명히 생각하고 있는 거 같아.

Note

• **hold** : 무언가를 쥐고 있다

• **hold up** : 견디다, 버티다, 무게를 지탱하다. 혹은, 기다리다(= **hold on**, **wait up**)

Practice

① 그녀가 잘 버티고 있는 것 같아?

② 그가 얼마나 버틸 수 있는지 보자.

③ 나는 이제는 더 이상 못 버티겠어.

④ 지금까지 잘 버텨왔잖아.

주요 장면 STUDY

Monica Hey, hold on there, tiger. How's it going? **How you holding up?**

Monica 잠깐 이리 와봐. 어때? 잘되고 있어?

Joey Well, not so good. She <u>definitely</u> thinks tonight is the night we're gonna <u>complete</u> the <u>transaction</u>, if you know what I.

Joey 글쎄, 감이 안 좋아. 그녀가 오늘 밤 우리 관계를 완성할 거라고 분명히 생각하고 있는 거 같아.

Joey Then you do. Heh, heh.

Joey 무슨 말인지 알지?

Monica So, uh, have you ever thought about being there for her?

Monica 그래서, 그녀를 위해서 같이 있어줄 생각은 안 해봤어?

Joey What do you mean?

Joey 무슨 소리야.

Monica You know, just be there for her.

Monica 있지, 그냥 같이 있어주라고.

Joey Not following you.

Joey 모르겠는데.

Monica Think about it.

Monica 생각해봐.

- hold up : 견디다, 버티다
- How(are) you holding up? : 어려운 상황에서 '잘 지내고 있냐'라고 물을 때
- definitely : 분명히, 틀림없이
- complete : 완성하다
- transaction : 거래, 매매

cost a fortune

큰돈이 들다

> **Phoebe** Oh, it's so pretty. **This must have cost him a fortune.**
>
> **Phoebe** 와, 진짜 예쁘다. 비싸게 줬겠는데.
>
> **Monica** I can't believe he did this.
>
> **Monica** 오빠가 이런 면이 있었네.

📝 Note

- **cost** : 돈, 시간, 노력 등이 들다(예 cost money, cost time, cost efforts)
- **fortune** : 전 재산(그 정도로 엄청 비싼 비용)
- **cost a fortune = cost an arm and a leg** : 큰돈이 들다, 정말 비싸다

⏱ Practice

1 너 이 차 고장 내면 정말 큰돈이 들 거야.

2 얼마나 돈이 많이 들든 내가 사줄게.

3 그거 얼마 줬어? 되게 비쌌겠다!

4 이 집을 사려고 정말 큰돈을 줬어.

주요 장면 STUDY

Phoebe Oh, it's so pretty. **This must have cost him a fortune**.

Phoebe 와, 진짜 예쁘다. 비싸게 줬겠는데.

Monica I can't believe he did this.

Monica 오빠가 이런 면이 있었네.

Chandler Come on, Ross? Remember back in college, when he fell in love with Carol and bought her that <u>ridiculously</u> expensive crystal duck?

Chandler Ross 말이야? 학교 다닐 때, Carol하고 사랑에 빠졌을 때 터무니없이 비싼 크리스탈 오리도 사줬던 애야.

Rachel What did you just say?

Rachel 방금 뭐라고?

- cost someone a fortune : ~에게 큰돈이 들다
- ridiculously : 말도 안 되게, 터무니없이

mind
신경 쓰다, 상관하다

> Joey Well, <u>given that</u> he's <u>desperately</u> in love with you, he probably wouldn't **mind** getting a cup of coffee <u>or something</u>.

> Joey 뭐, 너한테 푹 빠져 있는 걸 고려하면, 아마, 커피 같은 거 한잔하자고 해도 좋아 할 거야.

> Rachel Ross? <u>All this time?</u> Well, I've gotta talk to him.

> Rachel Ross가? 지금껏 내내? 글쎄 얘기 좀 해봐야겠어.

📋 Note

- **mind** : ~를 신경 쓰다, 상관하다.(**Mind your own business**)

  🅔.🅰 Do you mind if I ~?(Can I~?) : 내가 ~해도 괜찮을까?

  Do you mind ⊜ - ing? Would you mind ⊜ - ing? : ~해줄 수 있을까요?

  I wouldn't mind ⊜ - ing : ~해도 괜찮다, 좋다.

🕐 Practice

1️⃣ 내가 운전해도 괜찮아.

2️⃣ 내가 운전해도 괜찮을까?

3️⃣ 소금 좀 전달해줄 수 있을까요?

4️⃣ 뭐 먹는 것도 좋을 것 같아.

주요 장면 STUDY

Monica I think this is so great! I mean, you and Ross! Did you have any idea?

Monica 좋을 거 같아. 너랑 Ross 말이야. 너 알고 있었어?

Rachel No! None! I mean, my first night in the city, he mentioned something about asking me out, but nothing ever happened, so I just. Well, what else did he say? I mean, does he, like, want to go out with me?

Rachel 아니, 전혀! 여기 처음 왔을 때, 나한테 언제 한번 데이트하자는 말을 하긴 했었는데, 그 후로 아무 일도 없었어. 그게서, 그기 말고 또 뭐라고 해? 나랑 데이트하고 싶대?

Joey Well, <u>given that</u> he's <u>desperately</u> in love with you, he probably wouldn't <u>mind</u> getting a cup of coffee <u>or something</u>.

Joey 뭐, 너한테 푹 빠져 있는 걸 고려하면, 아마, 커피 같은 거 한잔하자고 해도 좋아할 거야.

Rachel Ross? <u>All this time</u>? Well, I've gotta talk to him.

Rachel Ross가? 지금껏 내내? 글쎄 얘기 좀 해봐야겠어.

Chandler He's in China!

Chandler 걔 지금 중국에 있어.

Joey The country.

Joey 진짜 중국.

- given that ~ : ~를 고려하면
- desperately : 필사적으로, 절실하게
- mind : 신경 쓰다, 상관하다, 꺼리다
- or something : ~이거나 다른 거
- all this time : 지금껏 내내

gut feeling

직감

Rachel I don't know, I mean, this is just my <u>initial</u> **gut feeling**, but I'm thinking oh, I'm thinking it'd be really great.

Rachel 모르겠어. 이건 내 직감인데, 내 생각인데, 좋을 거 같기도 해.

Monica Oh my God, me too! Oh! Oh, we'd be like friends-in-law!

Monica 세상에, 나도 그래! 우리 그럼 사돈 친구네!

📝 Note

- **guts** : 내장, 소화기관, 본능. (내 안에서, 속에서 이야기하는 바)

- **have a gut feeling that~** = **get a gut feeling that~** = **My gut feeling is that~**

⏱ Practice

1 나 뭔가 잘못되고 있다는 직감이 들었어.

2 그가 거짓말을 한다는 직감이 들었어.

3 너의 첫 직감을 믿어야 해.

4 너의 직감이 늘 맞지 않을 수도 있어.

주요 장면 STUDY

Rachel uh, oh, you guys, you know, it's Ross. You know what I mean? I mean, it's Ross.

Rachel 아, 애들아, Ross잖아. 무슨 말인지 알아? 다른 사람도 아닌 Ross라고.

All Sure.

All 물론이지.

Rachel I don't know, I mean, this is just my <u>initial</u> **gut feeling**, but I'm thinking oh, I'm thinking it'd be really great.

Rachel 모르겠어. 이건 내 직감인데, 내 생각인데, 좋을 거 같기도 해.

Monica Oh my God, me too! Oh! Oh, we'd be like friends-in-law!

Monica 세상에, 나도 그래! 우리 그럼 사돈 친구네!

- initial : 처음의, 초기의
- gut : 내장, 직감
- gut feeling : 직감

behind someone's back

~모르게

> **Rachel** Come on up.
>
> **Rachel** 올라오세요.
>
> **Monica** **Behind my brother's back**? It's exactly the kind of crazy thing you won't be hearing from me.
>
> **Monica** 우리 오빠 모르게 남자를 만나? 이게 바로 네가 나에게선 절대 들을 수 없는 이상한 말일 거야.

📝 Note

- **behind someone's back** : 상대의 등 뒤에서, 상대가 모르게
- **talk behind one's back** : 뒷담화를 하다.
- **see someone behind one's back** : 상대 모르게 바람을 피다.
- **go behind one's back** : 배신하다, 등에 칼을 꽂다, ~몰래 일을 꾸미다, 뒤통수치다.

⏱ Practice

1 네가 내 험담을 하고 다닐지는 정말 몰랐어.

2 너 뒤에서 모두가 너를 흉봐.

3 남자친구가 나 모르게 다른 사람을 만나고 있었어.

4 나를 믿어도 괜찮아. 나는 절대 너를 배신하지 않을 거야.

주요 장면 STUDY

Rachel Who is it?

Rachel 누구세요?

Intercom It's me, Carl.

Intercom 저예요, Carl!

Rachel Come on up.

Rachel 올라오세요.

Monica <u>Behind my brother's back</u>? It's exactly the kind of crazy thing you won't be hearing from me.

Monica 우리 오빠 모르게 남자를 만나? 이게 바로 네가 나에게선 절대 들을 수 없는 이상한 말일 거야.

• behind someone's back : ~모르게

judge someone

누군가를 판단하다, 단정 짓다

> **Julie** You don't think **they'll judge** and <u>ridicule</u> me?
>
> **Julie** 날 헐뜯고 놀리지 않을까?
>
> **Ross** No, no, they will. I just. uh.
>
> **Ross** 아니야. 사실 그러긴 할 거야. 그런데도…

 Note

• **judge** : 🔵 판단하다, 단정 짓다 🔴 판사

• **judge someone** : 보통은 안 좋은 쪽으로 누군가를 판단하다, 편견을 가지고 보다

Practice

☐ 네가 나를 안 좋게 볼까봐 걱정했어.

☐ 우리는 절대 너를 판단하지 않을 거야.

☐ 우리는 다른 사람을 판단할 자격이 없어.

☐ 책의 표지만 보고 판단하지 마세요.

☐ 사람을 겉모습만 보고 판단해서는 안 돼.

주요 장면 STUDY

Man For God's sake, will you <u>let it go</u>? There's no Rachel!

Man 제발, 그만 좀 하라니까. Rachel이란 여자 몰라!

Ross Oh, hey, hey, I got that.

Ross 이거 떨어졌어.

Julie Oh, thanks, sweetie.

Julie 고마워, 자기.

Ross No problem. I cannot wait for you to meet my friends.

Ross 진심에. 빨리 친구들한테 소개시켜주고 싶어.

Julie Really?

Julie 정말?

Ross Yeah.

Ross 그럼.

Julie You don't think **they'll judge** and <u>ridicule</u> me?

Julie 날 헐뜯고 놀리지 않을까?

Ross No, no, they will. I just. uh.

Ross 아니야. 사실 그러긴 할 거야. 그런데도….

Both Can't wait.

Both 빨리 소개해주고 싶어.

Ross Come on, they're gonna love you.

Ross 괜찮아, 다들 자기를 좋아할 거야.

- let it go : 그쯤 해둬. 그만 좀 해.
- judge : 누군가를 판단하다, 단정 짓다
- ridicule : 조롱하다, 비웃다

Let's Practice 모범답안

Let's Scene 101 — track of time : 시간 개념을 잊다

1. I **lost track of** time. I think I might be late.
2. The party was so fun that I **lost track of** time.
3. We must not be late. **Are** you **keeping track of** time?
4. You should **have kept track of** time.

Let's Scene 102 — get into a weird area : 이상한 방향으로(이야기가) 흘러가다

1. I think you**'re getting into a weird area**.
2. I think we**'re getting into a** dangerous **area**.
3. Let's not **get into that area**.
4. I told you not to **get into that area**!

Let's Scene 103 — a knockout :(한 눈에 매혹될 정도로) 매력적인 사람

1. DiCaprio was **a knockout** when he was young.
2. She was **a knockout** in high school.
3. My makeup will make you look like **a knockout**.
4. Wow, this dress is **a knockout**.

Let's Scene 104 — mean something : 진심으로 말하다

1. When I said "I hate you." I **didn't mean it**.
2. You can call me whenever you want to. I **mean it**.
3. He said he wants to break up, but I know he **doesn't mean it**.
4. Please tell me you **don't mean it**.

Let's Scene 105 — grow up : 철들다

1. It's time for you to **grow up**.
2. Would you please **grow up**!
3. When are you gonna **grow up** and become an adult?
4. He **grew up** too fast.

Let's Scene 106 — spell something out for someone : 일일이 설명해주다

1. Can you **spell out** the problem to me?
2. You should **spell out** the process in the beginning.
3. Do I have to **spell out** my expectations to you?
4. I understood the situation. You don't have to **spell it out**.

Scene 107 — go down that road : 어떠한 길을 가다

1. I really don't want to **go down that road** again.
2. You are **going down that road** again!
3. I don't think you would want to **go down that road**.
4. Before we **go down that road**, let's think about other options.

Scene 108 — a big step : 큰 발전, 도약

1. It was **a big step** for me.
2. Talking about yourself is **a big step**.
3. Today is **a big step** towards reaching our goals.
4. Graduating from college is **a big step** towards becoming an adult.

Scene 109 — a fling : 썸(진지하지 않은 관계)

1. They're just **having a fling**.
2. They **had a fling** a few years ago.
3. We never went out. It was only **a fling**.
4. I never thought it was **a fling**.

Scene 110 — move out : 이사하다(현재 집에서 나가다)

1. Are you planning to **move out**?
2. My landlord told me to **move out** by this month.
3. Korean people eat Ja-jang-myeon on the **move-in days**.
4. I can't wait to **move in**.

Scene 111 — out of sorts : 몸 또는 기분이 안 좋은

1. I've been feeling **out of sorts** lately.
2. Are you okay? You look **out of sorts**.
3. The news made me **out of sorts**.
4. I couldn't sleep well lately so I am a little **out of sorts**.

Scene 112 — make a move : 행동을 하다(작업을 걸다, 진도를 빼다 등)

1. This is not right. We have to **make a move**.
2. We have to **make a move** before it's too late.
3. Did he **make a move** on you?
4. Are you waiting for me to **make a move**?

Scene 113 — make a pass at someone : 수작을 걸다

1. Nobody ever **made a pass at** me.
2. I can't believe he **made a pass at** me.
3. Should I **make a pass at** her?
4. She **made a pass at** my friend.

Scene 114 **hit on someone : 수작 / 작업을 걸다**

1. He **hit on** me.
2. Did he **hit on** you, too?
3. He has been **hitting on** her since last year.
4. Can you please stop **hitting on** me?

Scene 115 **a pig : 많이 먹는, 더러운, 무례한, 말 안 듣는, 문란한 사람**

1. I'm sorry but your boyfriend is **a pig**.
2. You really have to stop being **a pig**.
3. I never said you were **a pig**.
4. Everyone thinks you are **a pig**.

Scene 116 **be there for someone : 곁에 있어주다**

1. I will always **be there for** you.
2. When you need a friend, I will always **be there for** you.
3. You **were** always **there for** me.
4. You **were there for** me when I was going through tough times.

Scene 117 **deserve something : ~를 받을 만하다**

1. You **deserve** a big reward.
2. You worked really hard. You definitely **deserve** it.
3. I don't **deserve** this much love.
4. I don't **deserve** you.

Scene 118 **only child : 외동**

1. Sometimes, it's lonely being an **only child**.
2. I like being an **only child**.
3. I've always wanted to be an **only child**.
4. I got all my parents' attention because I was an **only child**.

Scene 119 **better off : ~하는 것이 낫다**

1. I'm much **better off** now than last year.
2. I think I'm **better off** without him.
3. I think you would be **better off** living alone.
4. I think you would be **better off** if you start working.
   = I think you would be **better off** if you start earning money.

Scene 120 **big time : 엄청나게, 대단히, 완전히**

1. I owe you **big time**.
2. They messed up the performance **big time**.
3. The team lost the game **big time**.
4. I'm in love with you **big time**.

Scene 121　suck up to someone : 아부하다, 비위를 맞추다

1. He always **sucks up to** his boss.
2. I saw you **sucking up to** him.
3. I don't like **sucking up to** other people.
4. I'm never going to **suck up to** other people.

Scene 122　keep an eye on someone : 예의 주시하다, 감시하다

1. Would you **keep an eye on** my bag, please?
2. Could you **keep an eye on** my kid, please?
3. I'm **keeping my eye on** you.
4. I'm **keeping my eye on** the tech market these days.

Scene 123　come clean with someone : 솔직하게 털어놓다

1. I think you never **came clean with** me.
2. I want you to **come clean with** me.
3. I am waiting for you to **come clean with** me.
4. Sometimes it's hard to **come clean with** the people close to you.

Scene 124　all over someone : ~에게 관심을 주다

1. When she came out the door, the reporters were **all over her**.
2. I was scared when they were **all over me** to find out what happened.
3. She was **all over him** at the party.
4. I don't want to see you **all over her**.

Scene 125　end up :(결국) ~하게 되다

1. We **ended up** moving to the countryside.
2. I don't want to **end up** like you.
3. I knew you two would **end up** with each other.
4. His food **ended up** in the trash can.

Scene 126　bail on someone : 버리다, 떠나다, 바람맞히다

1. You'll regret **bailing on** me.
2. I will never **bail on** you.
3. Are you **bailing on** us?
4. I **bailed on** yoga class today.

Scene 127　set someone up with someone :(이성을) 소개시키다, 엮다

1. I really want to **set you up with** my friend.
2. Are you trying to **set me up with** him?
3. She **set us up**(on a date).
4. I never asked you to **set me up with** her.

Scene 128 It's on me : 내가 살게

1. Order anything you want. **It's on me**.
2. Do you wanna have dinner with me? **It's on me**.
3. Beer'**s on me**.
4. Coffee'**s on me**.
5. Next round **is on me**. Okay?

Scene 129 go for : ~를 하다, 시도하다, 선택하다

1. I'll **go for** an ice latte.
2. Do you wanna **go for** a walk with me?
3. I thought about it, and I've decided to **go for** it.
4. I think you can do it. **Go for** it!

Scene 130 happened to : 우연히 ~하게 되다

1. You **happened to** call at the right moment.
2. I **happened to** see you crying.
3. I **happened to** see your text.
4. I **happened to** be away when you called.

Scene 131 in the first place : 애초에

1. We shouldn't have started it **in the first place**.
2. I shouldn't have told you **in the first place**.
3. I don't understand why you chose this job **in the first place**.
4. **In the first place**, this is none of your business.

Scene 132 get on with one's life :(원래 방식대로) 자기 삶을 살아가다

1. It's time for you to **get on with your life**.
2. I'm slowly **getting on with my life**.
3. I'm happy that she is **getting on with her life**.
4. When are you going to **get on with your life**?

Scene 133 at the end of the day : 종국에는

1. Thank you for your advice, but **at the end of the day**, it's my decision.
2. **At the end of the day**, you have to choose what's best for you.
3. **At the end of the day**, you will be the winner.
4. **At the end of the day**, it'll all be worth it.

Scene 134 keep it down : 조용히 하다, 목소리를 낮추다

1. Can you please **keep it down**? I'm on the phone.
2. Can you please **keep it down**? I'm trying to study!
3. Mom told us to **keep it down**.
4. We should **keep it down** in front of him.

take someone by surprise : ~를 깜짝 놀라게 하다

1. To be honest, your reaction **took me by surprise**.
2. He **took me by surprise** when he showed up at my work.
3. Her announcement **took all of us by surprise**.
4. Sudden rain **took us by surprise**.

root for : 를 응원하다

1. Which team are you **rooting for**?
2. Which candidate are you **rooting for**?
3. No matter what, we're always **rooting for** you.
4. I've always **rooted for** you to succeed.

put a roof over someone's head : 거처를 마련해주다

1. We're so lucky that we **have a roof over our head**.
2. We're not rich, but at least we **have a roof over our head**.
3. I wish I **had a roof over my head**.
4. Don't forget that I **put a roof over your head**.

spoil someone's appetite : 입맛을 잃게 하다

1. Don't give him candy. It'll **spoil his appetite**.
2. I won't eat it. I don't wanna **spoil my appetite**.
3. You just **spoiled my appetite**.
4. The movie **spoiled my appetite**.

cuddle : 꼭 껴안다

1. I won't do anything. I just want to **cuddle**.
2. I saw you guys **cuddling**.
3. I love to **cuddle** my cat.
4. He still needs something to **cuddle** when he sleeps.

how come : 왜? 어쩌다가?

1. **How come** you are not coming?
2. **How come** you never call me first?
3. **How come** you are not eating?
4. **How come** she didn't come to class today?

in a row : 연속으로, 연달아서

1. He won 5 times **in a row**.
2. He didn't come to work 3 days **in a row**.
3. I have 3 exams / 3 meetings **in a row** today.
4. I can have kimchi-jjigae 7 days **in a row**.

Let's Scene 142 　catch someone : 따라잡다, 만나다

1. I still have some work to do, so I'll **catch you** at home.
2. You can leave first. I'll **catch you**.
3. I have to go. Can I **catch you** later?
4. You won't be able to **catch me** at work after 6pm.

Let's Scene 143 　grow apart :(크면서) 사이가 멀어지다

1. We **grew apart** as we got older.
2. We **grew apart** after I moved away.
3. Childhood friends eventually **grow apart**.
4. Don't worry. We'll never **grow apart**.

Let's Scene 144 　miss out(on ~) :(중요한 것을) 놓치다

1. This is a really great opportunity. Don't **miss out**!
2. Don't **miss out** on this week's party.
3. I'm so sad that I **missed out** on seeing him.
4. You don't wanna **miss out** on our next class.

Let's Scene 145 　lay off : 해고하다, 그만두다

1. I got **laid off**.
2. The **lay off** isn't your fault.
3. The company is **laying off** 10% of their employees.
4. I had to **lay off** many people today.

Let's Scene 146 　now that : 이제 ~하게 되었으니, ~하니까

1. **Now that** I'm working, I can buy you dinner.
2. **Now that** it stopped raining, we can walk home.
3. **Now that** the exams are over, I can sleep as much as I want!
4. **Now that** I think about it, you are right.

Let's Scene 147 　sit around : 빈둥거리다, ~하며 세월을 보내다

1. I like to just **sit around**.
2. We don't have time to **sit around** like this.
3. I'm not just **sitting around**. I'm thinking!
4. If you are going to **sit around** like this, just go home.

Let's Scene 148 　occur to someone : ~에게 갑자기 생각이 들다

1. It **occurred to** me that I'm still young.
2. It **occurred to** me that we don't have much time.
3. Did it not **occur to** you to call me?
4. It didn't **occur to** me that you would be worried.

Scene 149　get a raise : 월급이 오르다

1. I wish I could **get a raise**.
2. I thought I was **getting a raise** this year.
3. I think it's about time for me to **get a raise**.
4. You'll **get a raise** this month.

Scene 150　might as well : ~하는 게 낫다, ~하는 것도 나쁘지 않다

1. We **might as well** wait for him.
2. You **might as well** do what you want.
3. If you can't avoid it, **might as well** enjoy it!
4. There's nothing to lose. You **might as well** ask her out.

Scene 151　odds of : ~할 가능성

1. **The odds are** that it may rain today.
2. **The odds are** that he may not recover.
3. What are **the odds of** meeting someone you know here?
4. **The odds of** winning the lottery are quite low.

Scene 152　any minute(now) : 곧, 당장이라도, 금방이라도

1. Hurry up! They'll be here **any minute**.
2. The bus will arrive **any minute** now.
3. It looks like it may rain at **any minute**.
4. This house looks like it might collapse at **any minute** now.

Scene 153　be around : 근처에 있다, 옆에 있다

1. I think I'll **be around** for about an hour.
2. Will you **be around** tomorrow?
3. I don't want you to **be around** her.
4. He is really fun to **be around**.

Scene 154　make up for : 만회하다, 화해하다

1. Give me a chance to **make up for** my mistake.
2. You still have time to **make up for** your mistake.
3. Do whatever you can to **make up for** the loss.
4. Let me pay for dinner to **make up for** being late.

Scene 155　be spoiled : 버릇없는, 오냐오냐 큰

1. I don't like him because he's so **spoiled**.
2. I know that I'm **spoiled**.
3. The kids **are** already so **spoiled**.
4. I **was** so **spoiled** that day.

Scene 156   stand someone up : 바람맞히다

1. I think he **stood me up**.
2. I'm so sorry that I **stood you up** the other day.
3. Are you going to **stand me up** again?
4. No, I promise I will never **stand you up** again.

Scene 157   be nuts / nutsy about : 굉장히 좋아하다

1. I'm really **nutsy about** sports.
2. He **is** really **nutsy about** movies.
3. I know that he **is nutsy about** me.
4. I don't care if he **is nutsy about** me.

Scene 158   worst case scenario : 최악의 경우에

1. **Worst case scenario**, we might not be able to go home.
2. **Worst case scenario**, you might lose everything.
3. I think we should think of **the worst-case scenario**.
4. **The worst-case scenario** here is that we have to walk home.

Scene 159   get over : 극복하다, 잊다(~로부터 회복하다)

1. I'm trying to **get over** him.
2. I thought I **got over** him, but maybe not.
3. It's been a year, and you still can't **get over** her?
4. I don't think I can ever **get over** her.

Scene 160   run low(on) : ~가 모자라다, 고갈되다

1. I think we're **running low on** gas.
2. We are **running low on** time.
3. They are **running low on** clean water.
4. We will soon **run low on** resources.

Scene 161   for real : 진짜로, 진지하게

1. You quit your job? **For real**?
2. We are playing **for real**.
3. You are just pretending. You're not doing it **for real**.
4. I'm gonna do it **for real** this time.

Scene 162   bluff : 허세를 부리다

1. Don't worry. He's just **bluffing**.
2. I know you're just **bluffing**.
3. I told you I wasn't **bluffing**.
4. That's more of a **bluff** than a confidence.

Let's Scene 163 — owe someone something : 갚을 빚이 있다

1. You **owe me $20** for lunch.
2. Do I **owe you anything** else?
3. I **owe you dinner** for teaching me English.
4. I think you **owe me an explanation**.

Let's Scene 164 — beg to differ : 생각이 다르다

1. This has nothing to do with you.
   I **beg to differ**.
2. I think we should stop this project.
   I **beg to differ**.
3. I think he is the best singer in the world.
   I **beg to differ**.
4. She says that she can do it by herself, but I **beg to differ**.

Let's Scene 165 — give something a go : 시도해보다

1. I've never done it before, but I'll **give it a go**.
2. I don't know if I can't do it, but I'll **give it a go**.
3. I'm not very good at playing games, but I'll **give it a go** this time.
4. Why don't you just **give it a go**?

Let's Scene 166 — step on someone's point : 다른 사람이 말하는데 끼어들다, 상대의 말을 무시하다

1. Can you **stop stepping on my point**?
2. I tried to finish my story, but she kept on **stepping on my point**.
3. It's rude to **step on other's point**.
4. I don't like to **step on other's points**.

Let's Scene 167 — be full of it : 허풍 떨다, 말이 안 되는 소리를 하다

1. I don't like people who **are full of it**.
2. Do you believe her? She's totally **full of it**!
3. He claims to be a millionaire but I think he's just **full of it**.
4. To be honest, I thought you **were** just **full of it**.

Let's Scene 168 — be in disbelief : 믿을 수가 없다

1. She looked at me **in** complete **disbelief**.
2. We stared at each other **in disbelief**.
3. I understand that you would **be in disbelief**.
4. I shook my head **in disbelief**.

Let's Scene 169 — go with : 어울리다

1. Your shirt **goes well with** your shoes.
2. I think these earrings would **go well with** your dress.
3. Hamburgers **go well with** French fries.
4. Spicy rice cake and fried food **go well** together.

Scene 170 · run something by someone : (상대의) 생각을 물어보다

1. I think we should **run this by** our boss first.
2. Why don't you **run it by** your parents?
3. Please **run it by** me before you submit it.
4. I should have **run it by** you.

Scene 171 · say something to oneself : 속으로 생각하다, 혼잣말하다

1. I think she just **said something to herself**.
2. What did you **say to yourself**?
3. I think you should **say that to yourself**.
4. I kept **saying to myself** that I can do it.

Scene 172 · on purpose : 일부러, 의도적으로

1. I really didn't do it **on purpose**.
2. Are you avoiding me **on purpose**?
3. You keep running into me **on purpose**."
4. I didn't slam the door **on purpose**.

Scene 173 · be hard on someone : ~에게 심하게 대하다, 야박하게 굴다

1. Don't **be** so **hard on** him. He is still a kid.
2. I think our parents **were** pretty **hard on** us.
3. Don't **be** so **hard on** yourself.
4. I **was hard on** you because you had talent.

Scene 174 · needy : 징징거리는, 애정을 갈구하는

1. Can you stop being so **needy**?
2. I can't handle him because he is so **needy**.
3. I don't want to be the **needy** one.
4. I won't be **needy** anymore if you help me this one time.

Scene 175 · on the other line : 통화 중이다

1. I tried to call you but you were **on the other line**.
2. Why are you always **on the other line**?
3. He isn't answering. I think he's **on the other line**.
4. I'm **on the other line**, so I'll call you back later.

Scene 176 · see someone : ~와 사귀다

1. I am **seeing someone** these days.
2. Why don't you start **seeing someone**?
3. Do you think he is **seeing someone**?
4. I have been **seeing someone** besides you.

Scene 177　can't help v-ing : ~를 하지 않을 수 없다, 어쩔 수 없다

1. I **can't help** think**ing** about my mistake.
2. I **can't help** think**ing** about you.
3. He was so handsome that I **couldn't help** look**ing** at him.
4. I **couldn't help** listen**ing** to their story.

Scene 178　run out on someone : ~를 버리다

1. I can't believe you **ran out on** me.
2. I won't forgive you for **running out on** me.
3. I **ran out on** my boyfriend when I found out that he was seeing someone.
4. His parents **ran out on** him when he was young.

Scene 179　lose it :(화, 웃음 등을) 참지 못하다, 이성을 잃다

1. Calm down. I think you are **losing it**.
2. I completely **lost it** when she blamed me for it.
3. If you ask me one more question, I might just **lose it**.
4. I tried to hide my emotions, but I eventually **lost it**.

Scene 180　get something : 이해하다

1. Do you **get** this question?
2. I don't think I **got** it.
3. Do you **get** why I am upset?
4. I **got** what you're saying.

Scene 181　make fool of oneself : 바보짓을 하다, 웃음거리가 되다

1. I think I'm **making a fool of myself**.
2. I'm not going to sing because I don't wanna **make a fool of myself**.
3. You are drunk and **making a fool of yourself**.
4. He **made a fool of me** in front of my friends.

Scene 182　show up : 나타나다

1. She didn't **show up** for work this whole week.
2. You're gonna be fired if you don't **show up** today.
3. She didn't **show up** until the movie ended.
4. I was surprised when you **showed up** on TV.

Scene 183　turn someone in : ~를 고발하다, 신고하다

1. I'm going to **turn you in**.
2. I really don't want to **turn you in**, but I have to.
3. I think you should **turn yourself in** before the police catches you.
4. I'm never going to **turn myself in**.

Scene 184 | take a moment : ~할 시간을 갖다

1. I think you should **take a moment** to calm down.
2. I think we should **take a moment** to think about our relationship.
3. I'd like to **take a moment** to review our past meeting.
4. I'd like to **take a moment** to introduce myself.

Scene 185 | pass for : ~로 통하다

1. She looks so young that she can **pass for** a teenager.
2. Do you think I can **pass for** 20?
3. You speak English really well. You can totally **pass for** a native.
4. She doesn't know anything about this field, and yet she **passes for** an expert.

Scene 186 | in / with reference to : ~와 관련하여

1. May I ask what this call is **in reference to**?
2. I'm writing this email **in reference to** your proposal.
3. I have something to tell you **in reference to** today's meeting.
4. **In reference to** that, I have nothing to tell.

Scene 187 | a touch : 약간, 조금

1. I think you are **a touch** out of control right now.
2. Can you add just **a touch** of sugar to my coffee?
3. I think yours is **a touch** sweeter than mine.
4. You are just **a touch** taller than me.

Scene 188 | used to : 예전에는 ~했다, ~하곤 했다

1. I **used to** be good at English, but not anymore.
2. I **used to** drink 10 cups of coffee a day.
3. We **used to** be close friends.
4. We **used to** see each other much more often.

Scene 189 | be in charge(of) ~ : ~에 대해 책임, 권한이 있다

1. I'm **in charge of** this office.
2. Who **is in charge of** this project?
3. She put me **in charge of** the Soybean Paste Stew.
4. I don't want to **be in charge of** anything.

Scene 190 | icky : 끈적한, 찝찝한

1. Don't touch that! It's kind of **icky**.
2. I think I got something **icky** on my shoe.
3. This food is **icky**. I can't eat it.
4. It's **icky** to go out with someone who's much younger than me.

Scene 191 | phone person : 통화를 좋아하는 사람

1. She is definitely not a **phone person**. She never answers the phone.
2. I know you are not much of a **phone person**, but just call once in a while.
3. I'm more of a text person than a **phone person**.
4. I'm not much of a **phone person**. Can we text instead?

Scene 192 | check up on someone / something : ~를 살피다, 확인하다

1. Please **check up on** the new employee often.
2. I came to **check up on** you.
3. I need to **check up on** some things first.
4. I called to **check up on** the project.

Scene 193 | cook something up : 꾸며내다, 지어내다

1. Let's **cook up** an excuse right now.
2. I think we **cooked up** a totally believable excuse.
3. You just **cooked that up**, didn't you?
4. Actually, that was just a **cooked-up** story.

Scene 194 | look out for someone : ~를 지키다, 보살피다, 조심하다

1. As an adult, you have to **look out for** yourself.
2. You're the older brother, so you have to **look out for** your sister.
3. You should **look out for** pickpockets in Europe.
4. Can you **look out for** a red car with me?

Scene 195 | hold up : 버티다, 견디다

1. Do you think she is **holding up** well?
2. Let's see how long he can **hold up**.
3. I cannot **hold up** any longer.
4. You've been **holding up** well until now.

Scene 196 | cost a fortune : 큰돈이 들다

1. It will **cost you a fortune** if you break this car.
2. I will buy it for you even if it **costs me a fortune**.
3. How much was that? It must have **cost you a fortune**!
4. It **cost me a fortune** to buy this house.

Scene 197 | mind : 신경 쓰다, 상관하다

1. I don't **mind** driving.
2. Do you **mind** if I drive?
3. Would you **mind** passing the salt?
4. I wouldn't **mind** getting something to eat.

Scene 198 gut feeling : 직감

1. I had a **gut feeling** that something was going wrong.
2. My **gut feeling** was that he was lying.
3. You have to believe your initial **gut feeling**.
4. Your **gut feeling** may not always be correct.

Scene 199 behind someone's back : ~모르게

1. I never knew you would talk **behind my back**.
2. Everyone talks about you **behind your back**.
3. My boyfriend was seeing someone **behind my back**.
4. You can trust me. I will never go **behind your back**.

Scene 200 judge someone : 누군가를 판단하다, 단정 짓다

1. I worried that you would **judge me**.
2. We will never **judge you**.
3. We have no right to **judge other people**.
4. Don't **judge a book** by its cover.
5. You should not **judge someone** by his or her appearance.